Classical Subjects Creativ

SONGSCHOOL LATIN

Book 1

More *free* audio pronunciation aids are available on the *Song School Latin Book 1* product pages at **ClassicalAcademicPress.com** (click the Support tab beneath the product photo).

AMY REHN

Song School Latin Book 1
© Classical Academic Press®, 2008
Version 2.0

Classical Academic Press
515 S. 32nd Street
Camp Hill, PA 17011

www.ClassicalAcademicPress.com

ISBN: 978-1-60051-499-9

Song School Latin Book 1 Music Credits:
Alec Nauck-Heisey: Guitarist & Vocals
Carolyn Baddorf: Violin & Vocals

Book cover and 3D illustrations by:
Rob Baddorf

Book design and illustrations by:
David Gustafson

PGP.08.24

Table of Contents

Audio File Information

	Audio File Number & Name		Chapter	Page	Time
Classical	1	Salve/Vale Song	1	1	1:26
	2	Latin Alphabet Song	1	1	0:37
	3	Vale Song	1	1	0:54
	4	Nomen Song	2	4	1:35
	5	Latin Vowel Song	2	4	0:43
	6	Quid Agis Chant	3	7	0:31
	7	Quid Agis Song	4	13	1:13
	8	Family Song	5	15	1:25
	9	Salve Song	6	18	0:36
	10	Silly Sally Chant	7	21	1:02
	11	Build a Casa	8	24	1:17
	12	Classroom Commands Song	10	32	0:37
	13	Classroom Commands Song (Cont.)	11	36	0:34
	14	Manners Song	12	40	2:25
	15	Animal Song	14	48	1:08
	16	Animal Song (Cont.)	15	51	0:32
	17	Christmas Chant	16	54	0:24
	18	Christmas Chant (Cont.)	17	58	0:14
	19	Action Song	19	66	1:13
	20	Action Song (Cont.)	20	70	1:12
	21	Edo Song	21	73	1:06
	22	Cibus Chant	22	76	0:21
	23	Canis Song	23	82	1:14
	24	Weather Song	24	85	1:34
	25	Seasons Song	25	88	0:47
	26	Caelum Song	26	91	0:35
	27	Row Your Navis	28	98	0:33
	28	Hortus Song	29	101	1:00
	29	Hiking Song	30	104	0:42
	30	Sailing Song	31	110	1:10

Audio File Number & Name		Chapter	Page	Time
31	Salve/Vale Song	1	1	1:27
32	Latin Alphabet Song	1	1	0:37
33	Vale Song	1	1	0:55
34	Nomen Song	2	4	1:35
35	Latin Vowel Song	2	4	0:43
36	Quid Agis Chant	3	7	0:31
37	Quid Agis Song	4	13	1:13
38	Family Song	5	15	1:25
39	Salve Song	6	18	0:36
40	Silly Sally Chant	7	21	1:02
41	Build a Casa	8	24	1:17
42	Classroom Commands Song	10	32	0:37
43	Classroom Commands Song (Cont.)	11	36	0:35
44	Manners Song	12	40	1:06
45	Animal Song	14	48	1:09
46	Animal Song (Cont.)	15	51	0:32
47	Christmas Chant	16	54	0:24
48	Christmas Chant (Cont.)	17	58	0:14
49	Action Song	19	66	1:13
50	Action Song (Cont.)	20	70	1:12
51	Edo Song	21	73	1:06
52	Cibus Chant	22	76	0:21
53	Canis Song	23	82	1:14
54	Weather Song	24	85	1:33
55	Seasons Song	25	88	0:47
56	Caelum Song	26	91	0:35
57	Row Your Navis	28	98	0:34
58	Hortus Song	29	101	1:00
59	Hiking Song	30	104	0:41
60	Sailing Song	31	110	1:10

Ecclesiastical

Classical Pronunciation

There are 24 letters in the Latin alphabet—there is no *j* or *w*. The letters *k*, *y* and *z* were used very rarely. Letters in Latin are never silent. There are two systems of pronunciation in Latin—classical and ecclesiastical.

Latin Consonants: Consonants are pronounced the same as in English with these exceptions.

Letter	Pronunciation	Example	Sound
b	before s or t like English **p**	**urbs:** city	*urps*
c / ch	always hard like English **k**	**cantō:** I sing	*kahn-toh*
g	always hard like English **g**oat	**gaudium:** joy	*gow-diyum*
gn	in the middle of the word like English **ngn** in ha**ngn**ail	**magnus:** big	*mang-nus*
i	before a vowel it is a consonant like the English **y**	**iaceō:** I lie down	*yah-keh-oh*
r	should be rolled as in Spanish or Italian	**rēgīna:** queen	*ray-geen-ah*
s	always like the **s** in the English **s**ing	**servus:** servant	*ser-wus*
v	always as an English **w**	**vallum:** wall	*wa-luhm*

Diphthongs: Diphthongs are two vowels with a single sound.

ae	au	ei	oe	ui
as in **eye**	as in **out**	as in **stray**	as in **coil**	not a diphthong; pronounced **oo-ee**

Latin Short and Long Vowels: Vowels can be short or long in Latin. When they are long, they have a little dash called a macron placed over them. Long vowels take about twice as long to say as short ones. (We will not be using macrons in this book, but the audio content will guide you so you pronounce vowels correctly.)

Short Vowels			Long Vowels		
Letter	Example	Sound	Letter	Example	Sound
a in Din**a**h	**casa:** house	*ka-sa*	**ā** in f**a**ther	**stāre:** to stand	*stah-reh*
e in p**e**t	**ventus:** wind	*wen-tus*	**ē** in th**ey**	**vidēre:** to see	*wi-dey-reh*
i in p**i**t	**silva:** forest	*sil-wah*	**ī** in mach**i**ne	**īre:** to go	*ee-reh*
o in p**o**t	**bonus:** good	*bah-nus*	**ō** in h**o**se	**errō:** I wander	*er-roh*
u in p**u**t	**cum:** with	*kum*	**ū** in r**u**de	**lūdus:** school	*loo-duhs*

Classical or Ecclesiastical Pronunciation?

Both pronunciations are really quite similar, so ultimately the decision is not a significant one. The classical attempts to follow the way the Romans spoke Latin (an older pronunciation) while the ecclesiastical follows the way Latin pronunciation evolved within the Christian Church during the Middle Ages, particularly within the Roman Catholic Church.

The main difference between the two pronunciations is the way *c/ch* and *v* are pronounced. The classical pronounces *c/ch* as an English *k*, whereas the ecclesiastical pronounces it (Italian style) as an English *ch* (as in check). The ecclesiastical pronounces *v* as the English *v* (as in victory) whereas the classical pronounces it as an English *w*. In the ecclesiastical, a *j* occasionally appears in place of an *i* and the *t* has a special pronunciation, like **ts** as in cats.

So, take your pick and stick with it! Either choice is a good one. Our audio and video files contain both pronunciations.

Ecclesiastical Pronunciation

There is no *w* in the ecclesiastical pronunciation of Latin. The letters *k*, *y*, and *z* were used very rarely. Letters in Latin are never silent.

Latin Consonants: In the ecclesiastical pronunciation, consonants are pronounced the same as they are in English with the following exceptions. The pronunciations specific to the ecclesiastical pronunciation have been shaded.

Letter	Pronunciation	Example	Sound
b	before s or t like English **p**	**urbs:** city	*urps*
c	before e, i, ae, oe and y always like English **ch**	**cēna:** food	*chey-nah*
c	before other letters, hard c like English **c**ap	**cantō:** I sing	*kahn-toh*
g	soft before **e, i, ae, oe** like English **g**erm	**magistra:** teacher	*mah-jee-stra*
g	before other letters, hard like English **g**oat	**gaudium:** joy	*gow-diyum*
gn	in the middle of the word like English **"ny"** in lasa**gn**a.	**magnus:** big	*man-yoos*
j	like the English **y** in **y**es	**jaceō:** I lie down	*yah-chey-oh*
r	should be rolled as in Spanish or Italian	**rēgīna:** queen	*ray-jeen-ah*
s	always like the s in the English sing	**servus:** servant	*ser-vus*
t	when followed by **i** and a vowel, like **tsee**	**silentium:** silence	*see-len-tsee-um*
v	always as an English **v**	**vallum:** wall	*va-luhm*

Diphthongs: With the exception of *ae*, which is pronounced "ay" in the ecclesiastical pronunciation, diphthongs are pronounced the same in both classical and ecclesiastical pronunciations. See the chart on the previous page for the other pronunciations.

Latin Short and Long Vowels: Vowels can be short or long in Latin. When they are long, they have a little dash called a macron placed over them. Long vowels take about twice as long to say as short ones. The ecclesiastical short and long vowels are pronounced in the same way as in the classical pronunciation. See the table on the preceding page.

Words to Learn

1. **salve** hello
2. **vale** good-bye
3. **discipuli** students
4. **magister** male teacher
   magistra female teacher

Chapter Songs

Salve/Vale Song [Audio File 1(C)/31(E)]
Here comes **magistra**,
Salve, **salve**!
Teach the **discipuli**!
Students, students!
Away goes **magistra**,
Vale, **vale**!
Good-bye, **discipuli**!
Good-bye, students!

Latin Alphabet Song [Audio File 2(C)/32(E)]
A B C D E F G (clap), H I J* K L M N O P (clap),
Q R S T U and V (clap), X Y Z (clap-clap).

Vale Song [Audio File 3(C)/33(E)]
Vale! **Vale**!
Time to go, time to go, **vale**.
It's the end of the day,
And time to say,
Vale, **vale**, time to go.

*The J is not in the alphabet used with the classical pronunciation, but is in the alphabet used with the ecclesiastical pronunciation.

Chapter Lesson

The Latin alphabet is just like our English alphabet except that it is missing one letter—**W**! This means it has twenty-five letters instead of the twenty-six we have. The letter **J** is used by those using the ecclesiastical pronunciation of Latin, but is not used by those using the classical pronunciation of Latin. Those using the classical pronunciation will just use an **I** in place of the **J**! You can hear how the Latin letters are pronounced by studying the pronunciation guide and by listening to your teacher or the audio content included with this book.

Practice Your Latin

1. Practice writing **salve** and **vale** by tracing the dots.

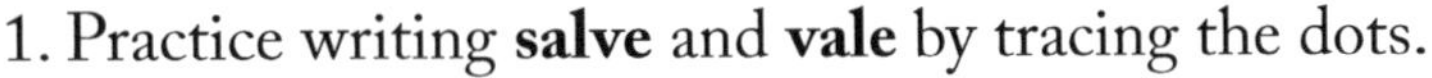

2. Practice writing letters A through H by tracing the dots.

A B C D E F G H

3. Draw a picture of your **magistra** or **magister** in the box below.

4. Practice saying "hello" and "good-bye" to each other and to your teacher in Latin.

Your **Magister/Magistra**

Grow Your English

The word "disciple" in English means "a follower." It was made out of a Latin word that you know! Which one of your new Latin words looks like the English word "disciple?" Circle one:

Vale **Discipuli**

Magister **Salve**

Chapter Story

Listen to your teacher read the story and fill in the blanks with either **salve** or **vale**.

This is Hare. ______________, Hare! He is fast and likes to run races. One day he challenged big, slow Tortoise to a race. This is Tortoise. ______________, Tortoise! As they began, Hare ran far away into the distance. ______________, Hare! After running so hard, Hare got tired and took a nap. While he slept, slow Tortoise caught up to him. ______________, Tortoise! When Hare awoke, he ran after Tortoise, but it was too late. All of the animals watched Tortoise come toward the finish line and shouted, "______________, Tortoise!" Hare was very sad that he lost and scurried down into his hole to hide. ______________, Hare!

Show What You Know

1. How do you say "hello" in Latin? ______________________

2. How do you say "good-bye" in Latin? ______________________

3. What is the word for "teacher" in Latin? ______________________

4. What is the one letter English missing from the Latin alphabet? ______________________

Chapter 2 Making Friends

Words to Learn

1. **Quid est tuum praenomen?** What is your name?
2. **Meum praenomen est…** My name is...

Chapter Songs

Nomen Song [Audio File 4(C)/34(E)]

Quid est tuum praenomen?
Quid est tuum praenomen?
Quid est tuum praenomen?
Tell me what your name is.

Meum praenomen est,
Meum praenomen est,
Meum praenomen est,
My name is __________.

Latin Vowels Song [Audio File 5(C)/35(E)]

A says **ah** and sometimes **uh**.
E says **ay** and sometimes **eh**.
I says **ee** and also **ih**.
O says **oh** and sometimes **ah**.
U says **oo** and also **uh**.
This is our Latin vowel song.

Chapter Lesson

There are five vowels in the Latin alphabet, just as in the English alphabet. The letter **Y** is never counted as a vowel in Latin. The Latin vowels work in the same way that English vowels work, and they even look the same. They make different sounds, though. You will have to work hard to remember the sounds they make! The more you sing the vowels song and listen to the audio content, the easier it will be. You can also chant through the sounds listed below to help you remember them.

A says **ah**, as in water and also **uh** as in Dinah.
E says **ay**, as in they and also **eh** as in pet.
I says **ee**, as in machine and also **ih** as in pin.
O says **oh**, as in clover and also **ah** as in pot.
U says **oo**, as in rude and also **uh** as in put.

Practice Your Latin

1. Practice writing your new words by tracing the dots.

Quid est tuum praenomen?

Meum praenomen est

2. Practice writing the Latin alphabet I through Q by tracing the dots.

I J K L M N O P Q

3. Write the Latin vowels for each sound.

ay ____ ee ____ oo ____ oh ____ ah ____ or ____

4. Match the English words to the Latin words.

good-bye	**salve**
What is your name?	**Meum praenomen est**
students	**vale**
hello	**Quid est tuum praenomen?**
My name is	**magistra**
teacher	**discipuli**

5. Speaking Latin, ask three people what their names are.

Show What You Know

For questions 1 to 4 below, circle A or B.

1. How do you say "What is your name?" in Latin?

   A. **Quid est tuum praenomen** B. **Meum praenomen est**

2. How do you say "My name is…" in Latin?

   A. **Quid est tuum praenomen** B. **Meum praenomen est**

3. When you leave you say:

   A. **salve** B. **vale**

4. When you come back you say:

   A. **salve** B. **vale**

5. The Latin alphabet is missing which letter? ___________

6. Circle the correct Latin vowel for each sound.

   a. ee A / I b. oh O / A c. ah U / A d. ay E / O

Chapter 3
How Are You?

Words to Learn

1. **Quid agis?** How are you?
2. **sum** I am
3. **bene** well/fine
4. **optime** great
5. **pessime** terrible

Chapter Songs

Quid Agis Chant [Audio File 6(C)/36(E)]

Hey, HEY! **Quid agis**?
Tell me how you are, friend.
Sum, sum! **Sum bene**!
I am doing fine, fine!

Hey, HEY! **Quid agis**?
Tell me how you are, friend.
Sum, sum! **Optime**!
I am doing great, great!

Hey, HEY! **Quid agis**?
Tell me how you are, friend.
Sum, sum! **Pessime**!
I am doing terrible!

Chapter Lesson

Did you notice that sometimes it takes fewer words to say something in Latin than in English? That is because of the special endings on many Latin words. These endings can mean "I" and "you" and many other things. The "s" at the end of the phrase "**Quid agis**" is the part that means "you." Endings on Latin words are like secret codes. You have to crack the code to find the word's real meaning.

Discipuli is a word that you learned in lesson one. I'm sure you remember that it means "students." What if you want to talk about only *one* student at a time, though? You have to change the sound at the end of the word. If you are talking about a girl student, the word is **discipula**. The vowel **a** sounds like **uh**. A boy student is a **discipulus**. Say the ending so that it rhymes with "fuss!" **Discipula** = girl student. **Discipulus** = boy student. Are you a **discipula** or a **discipulus**?

Grow Your English

An "optimist" is someone who always expects the best to happen. Circle the Latin word that sounds the most like "optimist."

Pessime **Salve** **Bene** **Optime**

Practice Your Latin

1. Practice writing vocabulary by tracing the dots.

Quid agis? Sum Bene

Optime Pessime

2. Practice writing the Latin alphabet R through Z by tracing the dots.

R S T U V X Y Z

3. Write the Latin word that describes how each person feels.

She looks like she feels ______________________.

She looks like she feels ______________________.

4. Draw a picture of your face and complete the sentence.

Sum ______________________________.

5. Ask three people how they are in Latin and then circle their responses.

Person 1:	**bene**	**optime**	**pessime**
Person 2:	**bene**	**optime**	**pessime**
Person 3:	**bene**	**optime**	**pessime**

6. Fill in the Latin word that fits best.

How do you feel when you get an ice cream cone? ___________________

How do you feel when you fall down and scrape your knee? ___________________

How do you feel when you are well? ___________________

Show What You Know

For exercises 1 to 4, circle the correct English word or phrase.

1. **Quid agis** means:	I am fine	How are you?	My name is
2. **Pessime** means:	terrible	great	well/fine
3. **Bene** means:	terrible	great	well/fine
4. **Optime** means:	terrible	great	well/fine

5. What does **sum** mean? ______________________________

Review

Circle the correct Latin word.

1. When you leave, you say: **salve** / **vale**.
2. When you arrive, you say: **salve** / **vale**.
3. The person who teaches you is a: **magister** / **discipulus**.

Chapter 4 Review

Master Your Words

Well, **discipuli,** you have learned about ten Latin words and three Latin phrases! Now it is time to take a week and make sure you have truly mastered your words. Can you give the correct English word for every Latin word below?

Chapter 1 Words

1. **salve** ______________________
2. **vale** ______________________
3. **discipuli** ______________________
4. **magister** ______________________
5. **magistra** ______________________

Chapter 2 Phrases

1. **Quid est tuum praenomen?** What is ______________________?
2. **Meum praenomen est…** My ______________________ . . .

Chapter 3 Words/Phrases

1. **Quid agis?** How ______________________?

2. **sum** ______________________

3. **bene** ______________________

4. **optime** ______________________

5. **pessime** ______________________

Master Your Songs

Salve/Vale Song [Audio File 1(C)/31(E)]

Here comes **magistra**,
Salve, **salve**!

Teach the **discipuli**!
Students, students!

Away goes **magistra**,
Vale, **vale**!

Good-bye, **discipuli**!
Good-bye, students!

Latin Alphabet Song [Audio File 2(C)/32(E)]

A B C D E F G (clap),
H I J K L M N O P (clap),
Q R S T U and V (clap),
X Y Z (clap-clap).

Vale Song [Audio File 3(C)/33(E)]

Vale! **Vale**!
Time to go, time to go, **vale**.
It's the end of the day,
And time to say,
Vale, **vale**, time to go.

Nomen Song [Audio File 4(C)/34(E)]

Quid est tuum praenomen?
Quid est tuum praenomen?
Quid est tuum praenomen?
Tell me what your name is.

Meum praenomen est,
Meum praenomen est,
Meum praenomen est,
My name is ____________.

Latin Vowels Song [Audio File 5(C)/35(E)]

A says **ah** and sometimes **uh**.
E says **ay** and sometimes **eh**.
I says **ee** and also **ih**.
O says **oh** and sometimes **ah**.
U says **oo** and also **uh**.
This is our Latin vowel song.

Quid Agis Chant *(See if you remember all the verses.)* [Audio File 6(C)/36(E)]

Hey, HEY! **Quid agis**?
Tell me how you are, friend.
Sum, sum! **Sum bene**!
I am doing fine, fine!

<u>Quid Agis Song</u> [Audio File 7(C)/37(E)]

Quid agis means how are you?
How are you? How are you?
Quid agis means how are you?
Su-um bene.

(The audio content provides additional verses with these final lines.)

Su-um tristis. ("I am sad.")

Su-um iratus. ("I am angry.")

Su-um optime. ("I am great.")

Activities

1. Match the Latin words to the English words.

Quid est tuum praenomen	How are you?
Meum praenomen est	Hello
Quid agis	What is your name?
Sum bene	Good-bye
Vale	My name is
Salve	I am well/fine

2. Circle the Latin word that fits.

   a. My teacher is a **discipulus / magister / magistra / vale**.

   b. My teacher teaches the **salve / magistra / discipuli**.

   c. The **discipuli / magister** should listen to the **discipuli / magister**.

Chapter Story

<u>The Three Little Pigs</u>

*Listen for the Latin words and circle them as your **magistra** or **magister** reads the story.*

Once upon a time, there were three little pigs. When they grew up, they left home to build their own houses. **Valete*** little pigs! The first little pig met a man who was carrying a bundle of straw. "**Salve**!" said the little pig. "**Quid est tuum praenomen**?"

The man answered, "**Meum praenomen est** Bob."

The little pig said, "Would you please give me some straw to build a house?" So Bob gave him straw and the little pig started building his house. When he was finished, he heard a knock at the door. "**Quid est tuum praenomen**?" he asked.

"**Meum praenomen est** wolf," said the wolf. "**Quid agis**?"

"**Sum optime**!" said the little pig.

"May I come in?" asked the wolf. But the little pig knew the wolf was bad, so he said, "Not by the hair of my chinny-chin-chin!"

"Then I will huff and puff and blow your house in!" said the wolf. And he did.

The second little pig met a man who was carrying a load of sticks. "**Salve**!" he said. "**Quid agis**?"

"**Sum bene**," the man replied.

"I would like to have some sticks to build a house," said the little pig. So the man gave him the sticks. When the little pig finished building the house, guess who knocked on his door? The big bad wolf!

"**Quid est tuum praenomen**?" asked the second little pig.

"**Meum praenomen est** wolf."

"You can't come in!" said the little pig. "Not by the hair of my chinny-chin-chin!" "Then I will huff and puff and blow your house in!" the wolf said. And he did!

The third little pig wanted a strong house. So, when he met a man who was carrying a load of bricks, he said "**Salve**! **Quid agis**?"

"**Sum pessime**!" said the man. "These bricks are too heavy for me! Would you like to have some of them?" So the third little pig built his house out of bricks.

Then the big bad wolf came along and knocked on his door. "Let me come in, little pig!" he said. "Not by the hair of my chinny-chin-chin!" said the little pig.

"Then I will huff and puff and blow your house in!" said the wolf. And he huffed and he puffed and he huffed and he puffed, but he could not blow that house in. He went away, and the little pig was safe in his house. **Vale**, wolf!

***Valete** is the way we say "good-bye" to two or more people.

Words to Learn

1. **pater** father
2. **mater** mother
3. **soror** sister
4. **frater** brother

Chapter Song

Family Song [Audio File 8(C)/38(E)]

My **pater** is really my father,
My **mater** is really my mom.
*My **frater** is my little brother,
And I am the **soror**, you see.

Pater, pater. Pater is really my father.
Mater, mater. Mater is really my mom.

(Repeat first verse.)

Frater, frater. Frater is my little brother.
I am the **soror**, and this is my family.

(*Repeat with: "My **soror** is my little sister, And I am the **frater**, you see.")

Chapter Lesson

The words in this chapter are very easy to learn. You can practice them every day when you talk to your family. Use the greetings that you have learned in Latin: **Salve, Mater!** or **Quid agis, Pater?** and **Vale, soror!** You can even greet a friend by name: "**Salve**, John! **Salve**, Susan!"

Practice Your Latin

1. Write the vocabulary words by tracing the dots.

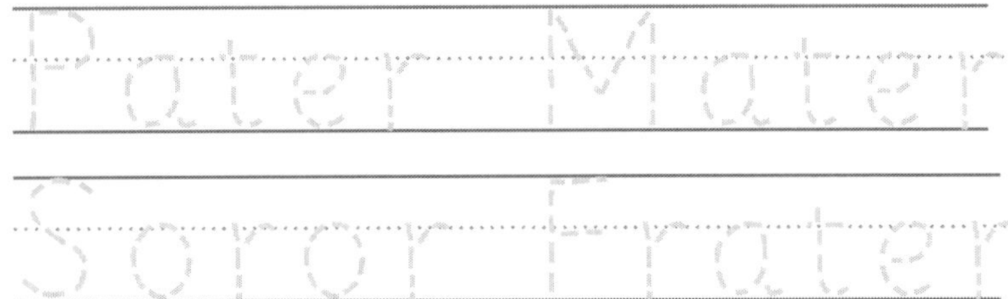

2. Match the pictures to their Latin names.

Pater

Mater

Soror

Frater

3. In the box below, draw a picture of your family doing something together and label each person with his or her Latin name.

Show What You Know

Circle the correct English word.

1. **frater**	brother	mother	sister
2. **soror**	brother	sister	father
3. **mater**	mother	father	sister
4. **pater**	mother	father	brother
5. **bene**	great	well/fine	father
6. **optime**	great	terrible	mother

Chapter 6 People

Words to Learn

1. **puella** girl
2. **puer** boy
3. **vir** man
4. **femina** woman

Chapter Song

Salve Song [Audio File 9(C)/39(E)]

When boys get up in the morning,
You say "**Salve, puer**!"
When girls get up in the morning,
Say "**Salve, puella**!"
(clap, clap)

Each boy grows into a man,
And then he is a **vir**.
Each girl grows into a woman,
She is a **femina**.
(clap, clap)

Chapter Lesson

Are you a **puer** or a **puella**? You know three words in Latin now that you can call yourself. You are a **puer** or **puella**, a **discipulus** or **discipula**, and you may be a **soror** or **frater**. The words in this chapter are a type called nouns. Nouns usually name a person, place, or thing. Can you think of any other Latin nouns that you have learned? How many nouns can you think of in English? There are too many to count!

Practice Your Latin

1. Write out the vocabulary words by tracing the dots.

Puella Puer

Vir Femina

2. Circle the correct Latin word.

My **pater** is a:	**puer**	**femina**	**vir**
My **soror** is a:	**femina**	**vir**	**puella**
My **frater** is a:	**vir**	**puer**	**puella**
My **mater** is a:	**femina**	**puella**	**puer**

3. Color and cut out the **vir, femina, puer** and **puella** and label with their Latin names. (See page 119 for larger cutouts.) Be ready to hold them up when the teacher calls the Latin words!

4. Draw lines to put the cookies in the right jar.

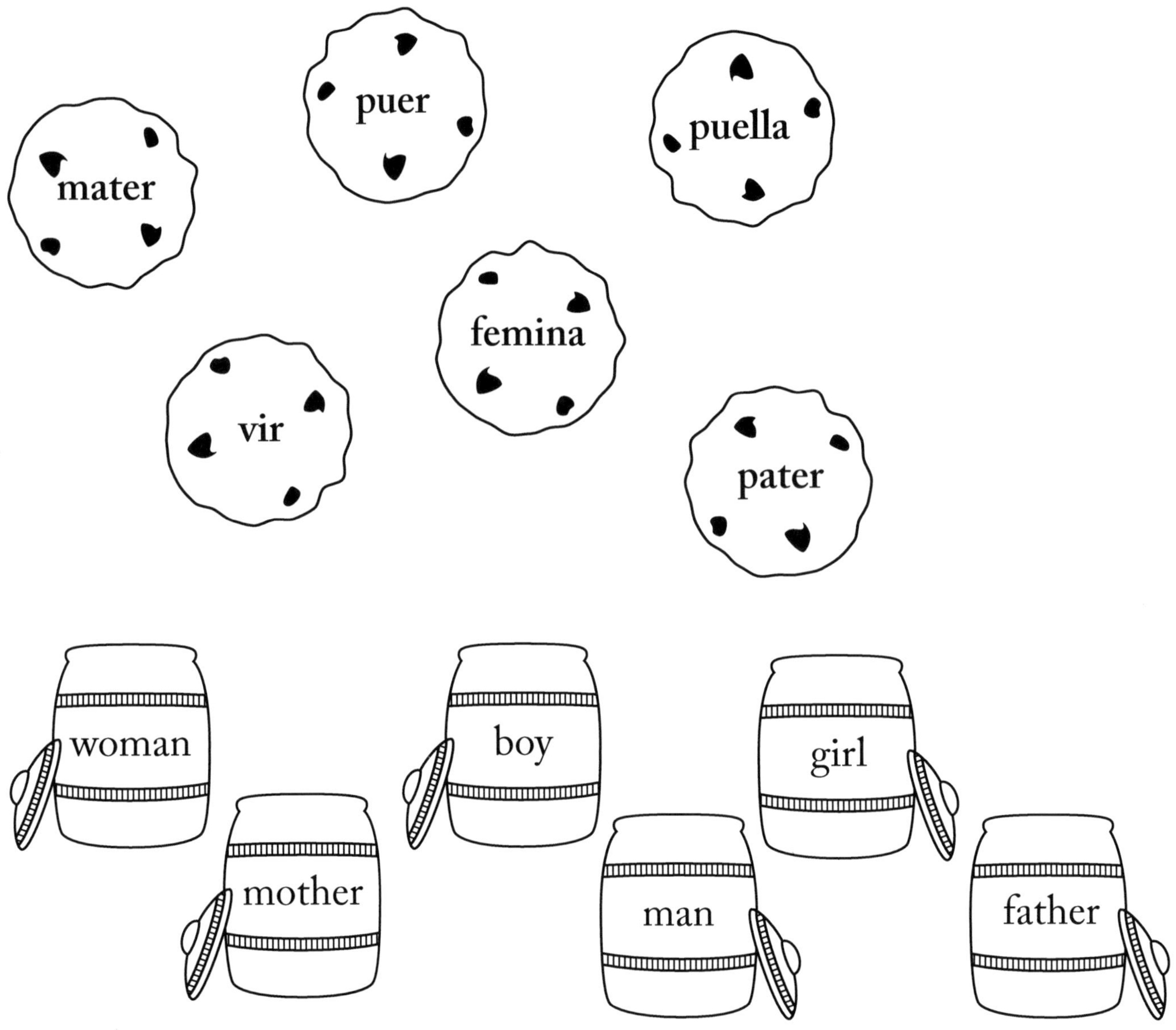

Show What You Know

1. Match the Latin words to the English words.

a. **femina**	boy
b. **vir**	woman
c. **puer**	girl
d. **puella**	man

2. Fill in the answer with the correct Latin word.

   a. My **pater** is a ________________________. b. My **mater** is a ________________________.

Words to Learn

1. **mensa** table
2. **sella** chair
3. **stylus** pencil
4. **liber** book

Chapter Song

Silly Sally Chant [Audio File 10(C)/40(E)]

Silly Sally sat in her **sella**,
Eating her curds and whey,
Along came Miss Molly and sat on the **mensa**,
But her **mater** chased her away.

Serious Sam picked up a **stylus**,
And started to write in a book,
Till Luke came along and looked at that **liber**,
And said "That's MY book you took!"

Chapter Lesson

Do you remember what we called the type of words in the last chapter? Do you think these new words are of the same type? Remember that nouns usually name a person, place, or thing. If you can touch it, you know it's a noun! Some nouns are things that you can't touch, though, like "song." Practice saying your new words aloud while touching each item that they name. You can call your desk a **mensa**.

Practice Your Latin

1. Practice writing your new words by tracing the dots.

Mensa Sella

Stylus Liber

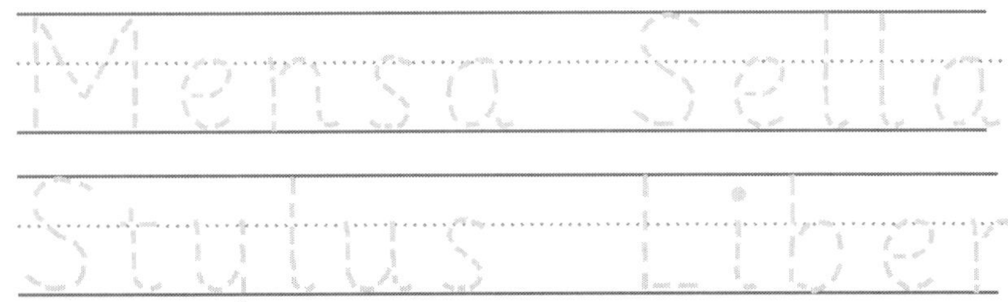

2. Color and cut out the pictures of these objects and label them in Latin (see page 121 for larger cutouts).

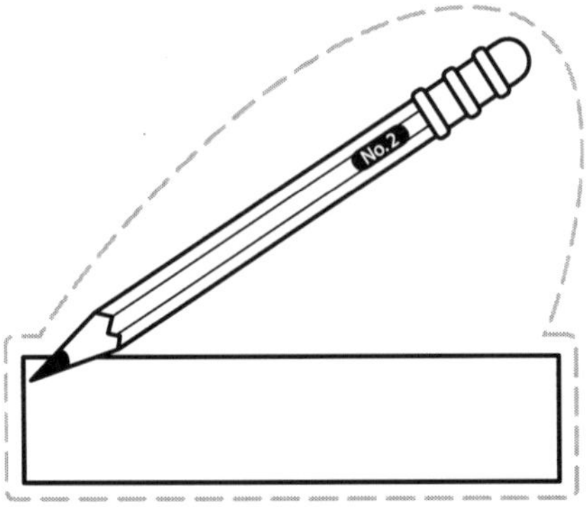

No.2

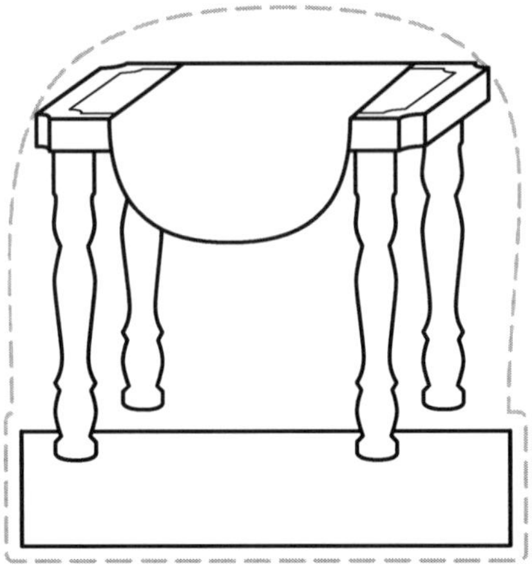

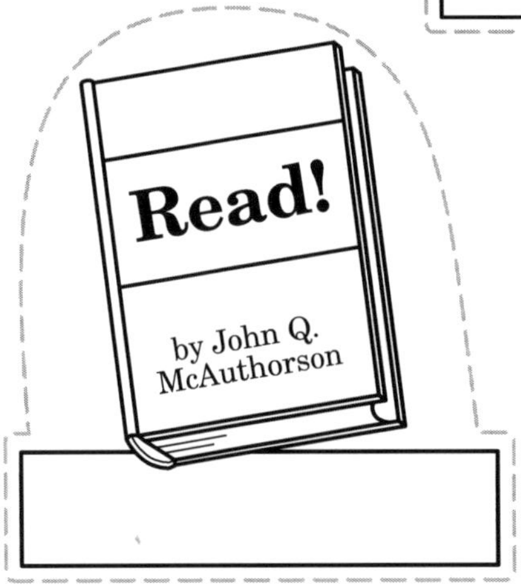

Read!
by John Q.
McAuthorson

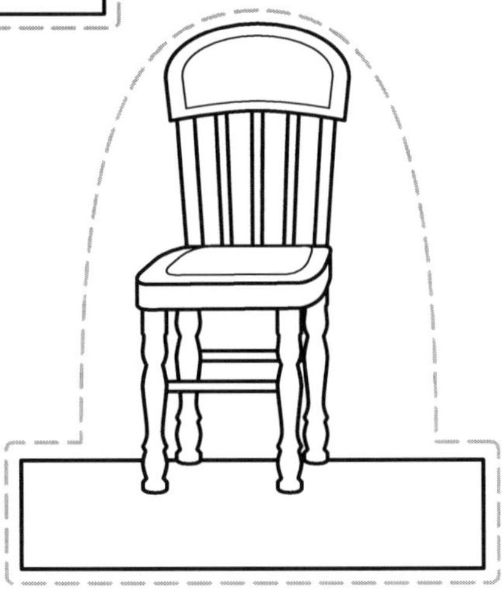

3. Circle your answer:

Should you sit on a **mensa** or a **sella**?	**sella**	**mensa**
Do you write with a **stylus** or a **sella**?	**sella**	**stylus**
Do you put your food on the **mensa** or on the **liber**?	**liber**	**mensa**
Do you read a **liber** or a **stylus**?	**liber**	**stylus**

Grow Your English

"Library" is an English word that was made out of one of these Latin words. Think about what you find in a library. Which Latin word do you think "library" came from? Circle your answer.

mensa **stylus** **liber** **sella**

Show What You Know

For questions 1 to 4, circle the correct English word:

1. **stylus** pencil table chair
2. **sella** table chair book
3. **mensa** book chair table
4. **liber** chair book pencil

For questions 5 to 6, circle the correct Latin word:

5. What Latin word did "library" come from? **sella** **mensa** **liber**
6. Tell me how you are in Latin: **Sum** **optime / pessime / bene**.

Chapter 8

Household Items

Words to Learn

1. **casa** house
2. **porta** door
3. **murus** wall
4. **fenestra** window

Chapter Song

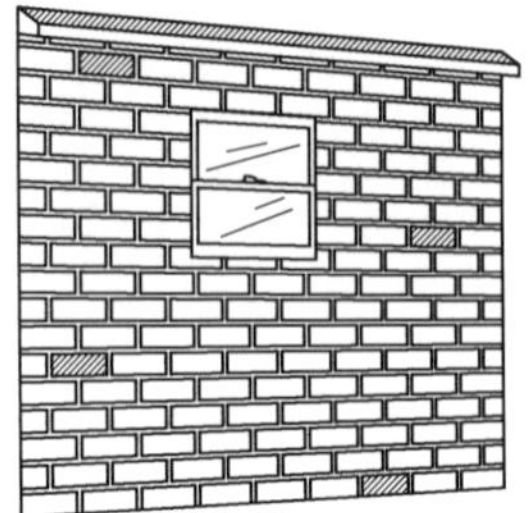

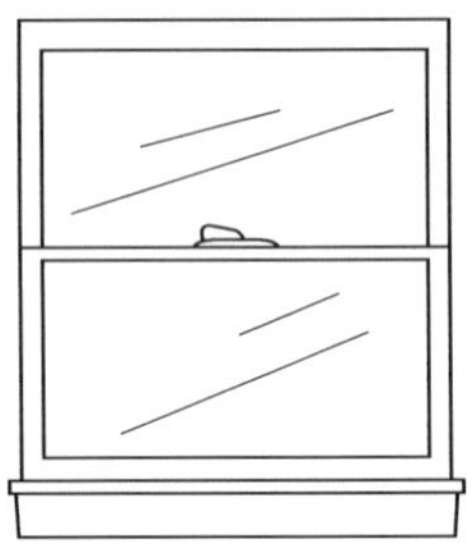

Build a Casa [Audio File 11(C)/41(E)]

Build a **casa**, build a **casa**,
Make it nice and tall.
Don't forget to paint the **murus**,
Paint the pretty wall.
Make a window, a **fenestra**,
Let in all the light.
And make a door, a great big **porta**,
Shut it tight at night.

Chapter Lesson

Can you touch all of the things named by our new Latin words? If so, what do you call this type of word? Latin nouns are grouped into five families. These families are called *declensions*. The Latin nouns that end with the letter "a" are in the first family, or the *first declension*. Can you pick out which of your new words are in the first declension?

Practice Your Latin

1. Practice writing your new words by tracing the dots.

2. Draw a **casa** on a blank sheet of paper. Label the door, windows and walls with the Latin words.

3. Build a **casa** with craft materials. Put Latin labels on the parts.

4. Choose the Latin word that fits best.

It's raining! Let's go into the __________________ (**casa/murus**).

There is a bird chirping! Look out the __________________ (**fenestra/murus**) to find it.

It's cold outside! Shut the __________________ (**murus/porta**).

I hung a painting on the __________________ (**murus/casa**).

Grow Your English

A castle is a huge, fancy house for a king. It came from one of the Latin words in this chapter. Say "castle" out loud. Circle the Latin word that it makes you think of.

fenestra **murus** **casa** **porta**

Show What You Know

Match the pictures to the Latin words.

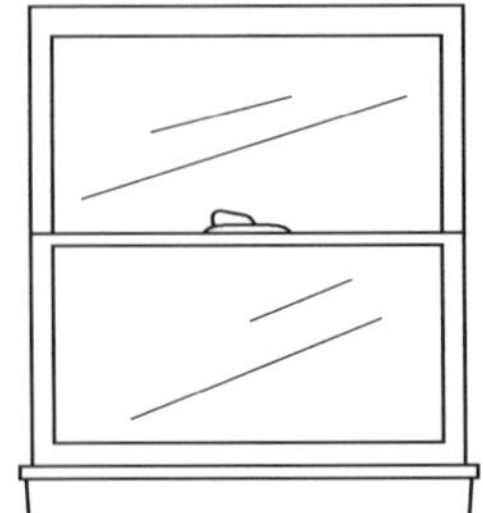

porta

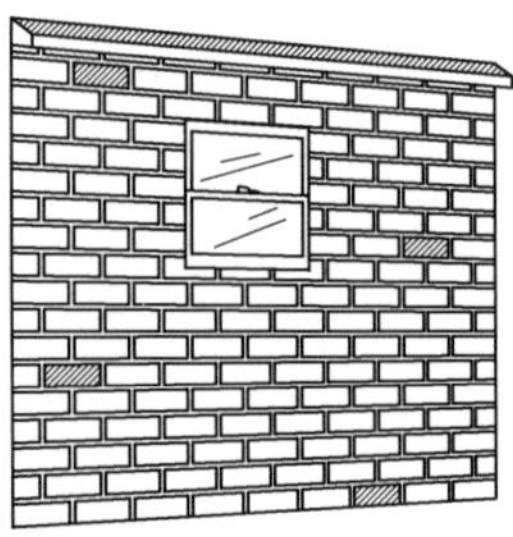

casa

murus

fenestra

stylus

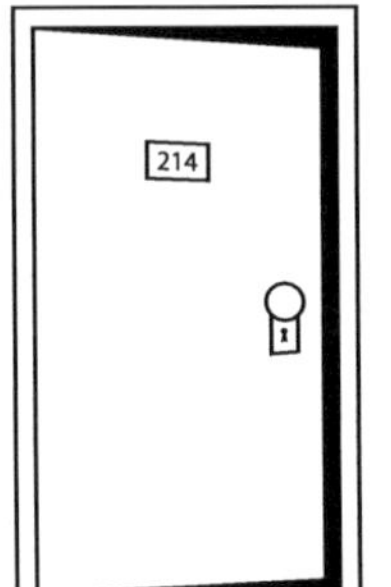

liber

puella

puer

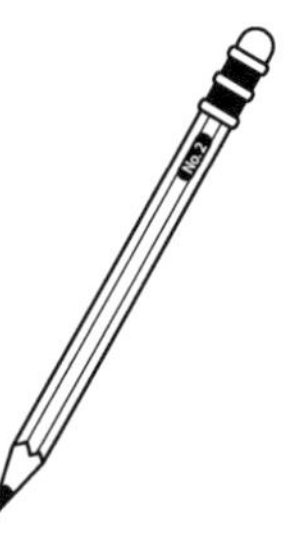

Master Your Words

Well, **discipuli,** you have learned another 16 Latin words! Now it is time once again to make sure you have mastered all 16 of your words. Can you give the correct English word for every Latin word below?

Chapter 5 Words

1. **pater** ____________________
2. **mater** ____________________
3. **soror** ____________________
4. **frater** ____________________

Chapter 6 Words

1. **puella** ____________________
2. **puer** ____________________
3. **vir** ____________________
4. **femina** ____________________

Chapter 7 Words

1. **mensa** ____________________

2. **sella** ____________________

3. **stylus** ____________________

4. **liber** ____________________

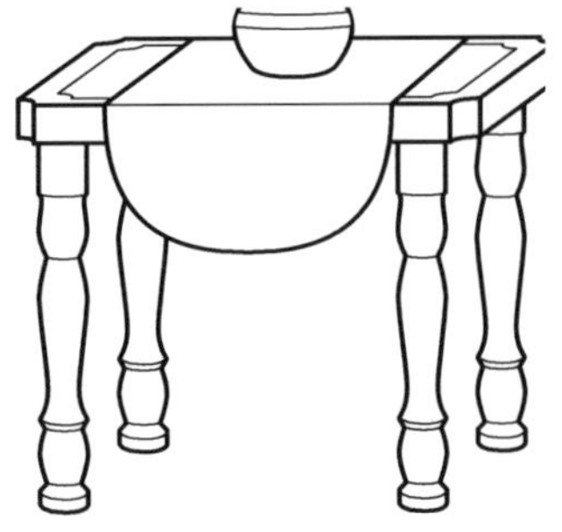

Chapter 8 Words

1. **casa** ____________________

2. **porta** ____________________

3. **murus** ____________________

4. **fenestra** ____________________

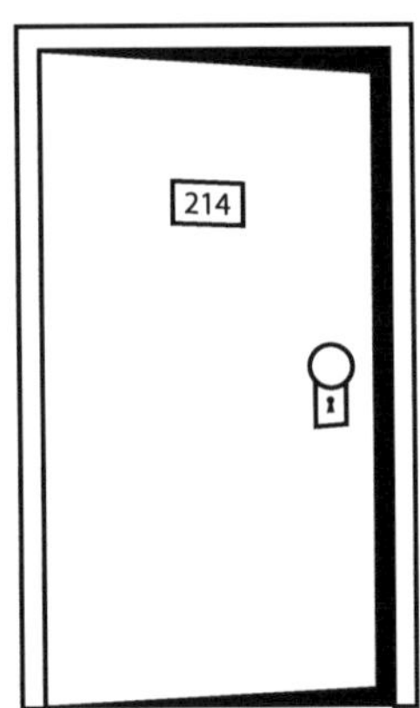

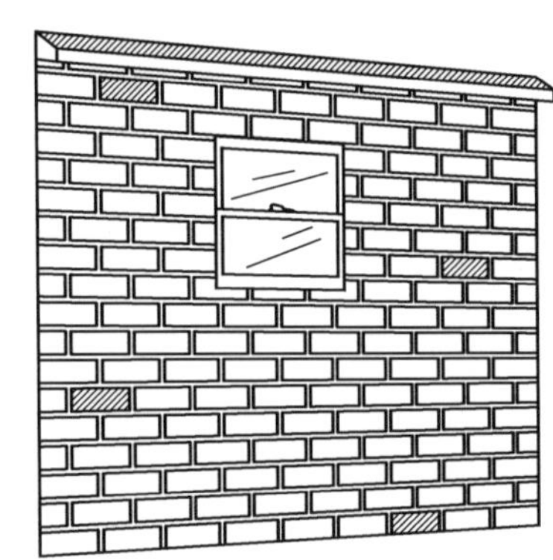

Master Your Songs

<u>Family Song</u> [Audio File 8(C)/38(E)]

My **pater** is really my father, My **mater** is really my mom.
My **frater** is my little brother, And I am the **soror**, you see.

Pater, pater. Pater is really my father. **Mater, mater. Mater** is really my mom.

(Repeat first verse.)

Frater, frater. Frater is my little brother. I am the **soror**, and this is my family.

(*Repeat with: "My **soror** is my little sister, And I am the **frater**, you see.")

Salve Song [Audio File 9(C)/39(E)]

When boys get up in the morning,
You say "**Salve, puer**!"
When girls get up in the morning,
Say "**Salve, puella**!"
(clap, clap)

Each boy grows into a man,
And then he is a **vir**.
Each girl grows into a woman,
She is a **femina**.
(clap, clap)

Silly Sally Chant [Audio File 10(C)/40(E)]

Silly Sally sat in her **sella**,
Eating her curds and whey,
Along came Miss Molly and sat on the **mensa**,
But her **mater** chased her away.

Serious Sam picked up a **stylus**,
And started to write in a book,
Till Luke came along and looked at that **liber**,
And said "That's MY book you took!"

Build a Casa [Audio File 11(C)/41(E)]

Build a **casa**, build a **casa**,
Make it nice and tall.
And don't forget to paint the **murus**,
Paint the pretty wall.

Make a window, a **fenestra**,
To let in all the light.
And make a door, a great big **porta**,
To shut up tight at night.

Activities

1. Match the Latin words to the correct pictures.

casa

pater

mater

porta

fenestra

murus

soror

frater

mensa

sella

liber

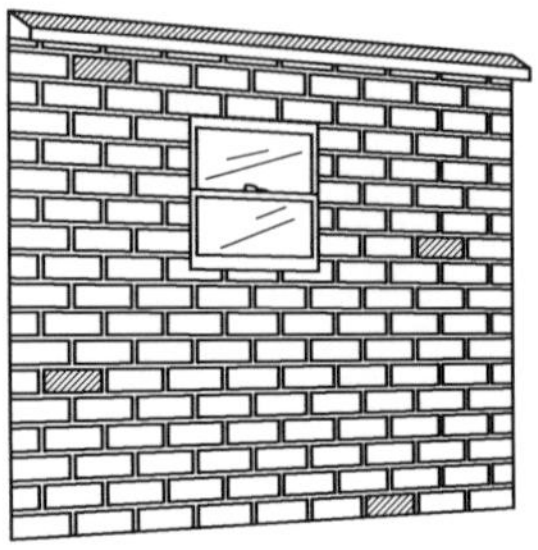

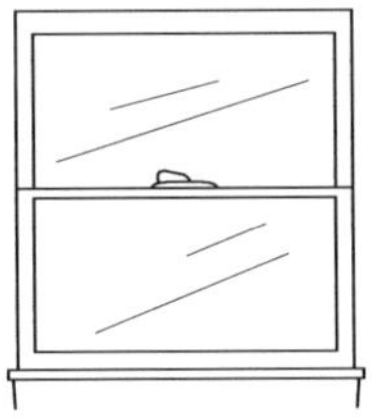

Chapter Story

<u>Goldilocks and the Three Bears</u>

Once upon a time, there was a **vir** and a **femina** who had a little **puella** named Goldilocks. She often worried them by wandering too far in the woods by herself. One day on a long walk she found a small **casa**. She went to the **fenestra** and peeked inside, but no one was there, so the little **puella** opened the **porta**, and went right in.

There was a **mensa** in the room, and sitting on it there were three full bowls of porridge. Goldilocks was hungry from her walk so she picked up the spoon of the first **crater** (bowl) of porridge and tasted it. "Ouch! It is too hot," she said. Then she tried the next **crater** on the **mensa**. "Yuck! It is too cold." So the little **puella** tried the last **crater**, and it was just right. "Yum."

After Goldilocks ate she was tired, so she walked through the **porta** to the living room to sit down. There were three chairs in the room, lined up along the **murus**. She went to the first **sella** and tried to climb up into it. "Err! This **sella** is too tall." So Goldilocks tried the second **sella**. "Ugh! This **sella** is too wide." Then she tried sitting in the last **sella**, and it was just right, but as she sat down it broke into pieces!

Goldilocks was upset and very sleepy now so she went upstairs to the bedroom to take a nap. There were three beds against the **murus** of the bedroom. She lay down in the first bed. "Oof! This **lectus** (bed) is too hard," she said. So she tried the next. "Oh! This lectus is too soft." So Goldilocks went to the last little **lectus** and lay down. It was just right and she took a nap.

While she slept, the owners of the **casa**, three bears, came home. The **Pater** bear was hungry and sat down at the **mensa** to eat. "Someone has been eating my porridge!" he yelled.

"Well, my, my, someone has been eating my porridge too!" said **Mater** bear.

"Well, someone ate all of my porridge!" cried the young **puer** bear. "My **crater** is empty!" So **Pater** and **Mater** bear shared their porridge with the **puer** bear, and they went through the **porta** to the living room to sit down. **Pater** bear growled and said, "Someone has been sitting in my **sella**!"

"Oh, honey," replied **Mater** bear, "Someone has been sitting in my **sella**, too!"

Then the poor **puer** bear shouted, "Someone sat in my **sella** and they broke it into pieces!"

So they went upstairs to rest in their beds, and **Pater** bear looked at his messy **lectus** and said, "Someone has been sleeping in my **lectus**!"

Mater bear gasped, "My heavens, someone has been sleeping in my **lectus**, too!"

But **Frater** bear yelled the loudest. "There is someone sleeping in my **lectus** right now!"

The little **puella** was terrified when she heard the yells and woke to find three big bears looking down at her, but **Mater** bear was kind and greeted her. "**Salve, puella. Quid agis?**"

"**Sum bene**," Goldilocks answered very quietly.

Pater bear said, "You need to go home to your own **pater** and **mater** now, the poor **vir** and **femina** must be very worried. You may come back again and play with **puer** bear, as long as you promise not to break another **sella**."

"Yes sir," the little **puella** squeaked. She went home but often made visits, with her **pater** and **mater**'s permission, to the little **casa** in the woods.

Chapter 10

Classroom Commands

Words to Learn

1. **sede** sit
   sedete sit (to more than one person)
2. **surge** rise/stand up
   surgite rise/stand up (to more than one person)
3. **scribe** write
   scribite write (to more than one)
4. **repete** repeat
   repetite repeat (to more than one)

Chapter Song

Classroom Commands Song [Audio File 12(C)/42(E)]

Sede, **sedete** in your seat,
In your seat, in your seat.
Surge, **surgite** on your feet,
Stand up on your feet.

Scribe, **scribite** write so neat,
Write so neat, write so neat.
Repete, **repitite**,
After me repeat.

Chapter Lesson

* Did you notice that your new words in this chapter are all commands? These words are *not* nouns. Your **magistra** or **magister** will give you instructions in Latin now. Be sure to learn these words well so you will know what to do when that happens! Listen carefully to the endings on the commands. If there is a "te" sound on the end, the command is to more than one person. If there is no "te" on the end, the command is for only one. The first form of the word in the list is the command to one person. Practice saying the words both ways. Remember to listen carefully to the ending when your teacher gives a command!

Grow Your English

"Scribble" comes from a Latin word. Think about what it means and say it aloud. Which one of your new Latin words does it remind you of?

____

Practice Your Latin

1. Practice writing your new words by tracing the dots.

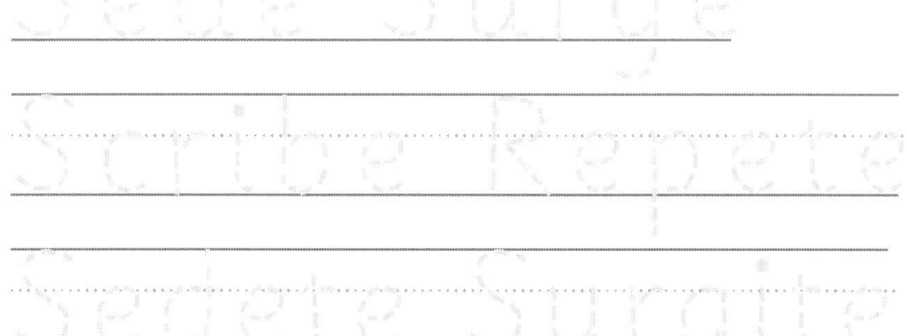

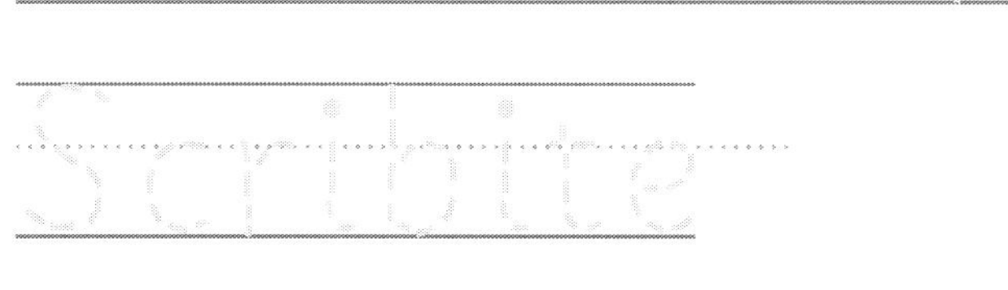

2. Match the Latin commands to the thing that you would use to obey each one.

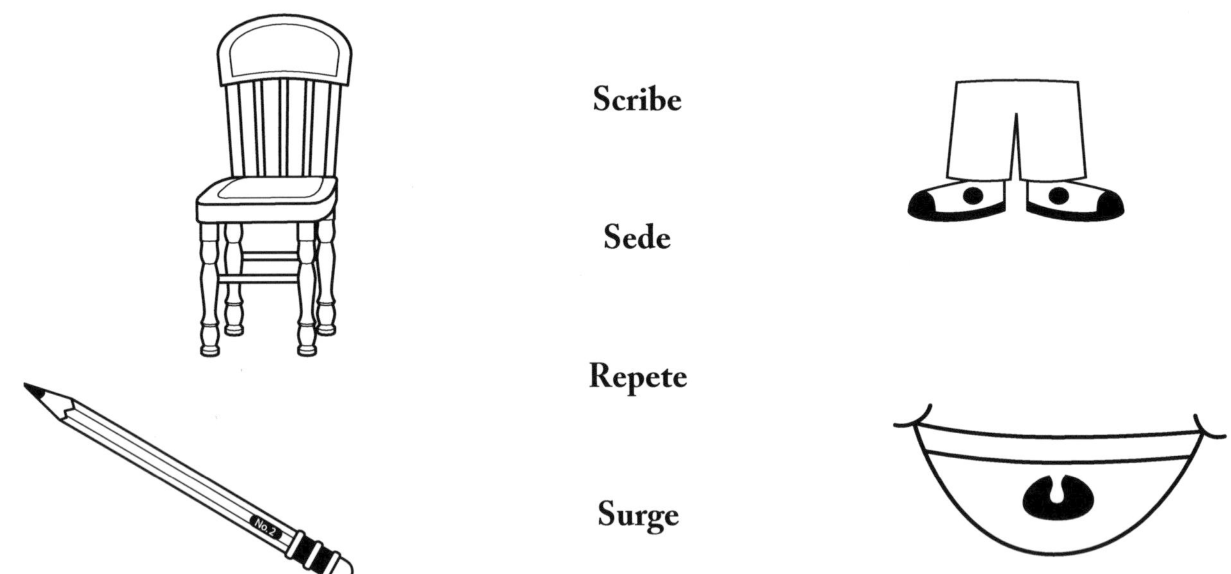

3. Practice time! Listen carefully and follow the commands that your teacher gives you in Latin.

4. Practice using the commands on three other people. Be sure to follow commands that others give you!

5. Are these commands to one person, or more than one? Circle your answer.

a. **sedete**	one	more than one
b. **surge**	one	more than one
c. **scribe**	one	more than one
d. **repetite**	one	more than one
e. **sede**	one	more than one

Show What You Know

1. What commands are these children obeying? Circle your answer.

a. 

sede **repetite** **surge**

b. 

repetite **scribe** **sede**

c. 

scribe **surge** **sede**

d. 

surge **scribe** **repete**

2. What Latin word does "scribble" come from? ______________________________

Chapter 11

More Classroom Commands

Words to Learn

1. **audi** listen
   audite listen (to more than one person)
2. **tace** be quiet
   tacete be quiet (to more than one person)
3. **aperi librum** open the book
   aperite libros open the books (to more than one person)
4. **attole manum** raise your hand
   attolite manus raise your hands (to more than one person)

Chapter Song

Classroom Commands Song (Continued)
[Audio File 13(C)/43(E)]

Tace, **tacete** - quiet please,
Quiet please, quiet please.
Audi, **audite** listen up,
Listen up to me.

Aperi librum – open the book,
Open the book, open the book.
Attole manum – raise your hand,
Raise it nice and high.

Chapter Lesson

This chapter has four more commands for you to learn! Do you remember how to tell if a command is given to more than one person? What sound do we put on the end of a command if it is for more than one person? "Te," of course! When a command is to only one person, you say that it is singular. Think of the word "single." It means "only one." If a command is to more than one person, you say that it is plural. So, **audi** is a singular command. **Tacete** is a plural command. See the "te" on the end of **tacete**? You have to listen a little harder to the commands that have two words in them. The "te" is on the end of the first word of the command. **Attole manum** is a singular command, and **attolite manus** is a plural command. What about **sedete** and **scribite**? Are they singular or plural?

Practice Your Latin

1. Practice writing your new words by tracing the dots.

Audi Audite

Tace Tacete

Aperi librum

Aperite libros

Attole manum

Attolite manus

2. Practice a few commands that your teacher will speak to you.

3. Circle the command that you think the teacher should give.

a. The students are not paying attention. **Attole manum**! **Audite**!

b. The students are talking out of turn. **Tacete**! **Aperite libros**!

c. The students need to practice writing their new words. **Audite**! **Aperite libros**!

4. Color the pictures. What commands are these children following? Match the pictures to the commands.

audi

tace

aperi librum

attole manum

5. Are these commands singular or plural? Circle the correct answer.

a. **sede**	singular	plural
b. **attolite manus**	singular	plural
c. **tacete**	singular	plural
d. **scribe**	singular	plural
e. **aperite libros**	singular	plural
f. **audite**	singular	plural

Grow Your English

The Latin word **audi** is the root of several words that you know in English. The word "audio" is talking about sound. You have probably heard it before. An "audience" is a group of people who are listening to some kind of sound. And the "auditorium" is the large room where you might see a concert or listen to a speaker. Latin is everywhere!

Show What You Know

Match the Latin words to the English words.

1. **attole manum**	listen
2. **tace**	open book
3. **audi**	raise your hand
4. **aperi librum**	be quiet

Review Words

Circle the matching English word.

1. **sede**	stand	sit
2. **scribe**	write	stand

Are these commands to one person or to everyone? Circle the correct answer.

3. **tacite**	one person	everyone
4. **surge**	one person	everyone
5. **audi**	one person	everyone
6. **sedete**	one person	everyone

Write your answer.

7. What Latin word does "audience" come from? ____________________

Chapter 12 Manners

Words to Learn

1. **amabo te** please
2. **tibi gratias ago** thank you
3. **ignosce mihi** excuse me

Chapter Song

<u>Manners Song</u> [Audio File 14(C)/44(E)]

When you ask for anything you have to say **amabo te**,
When you ask for anything you have to say **amabo te**.
If you really want to have it, don't just take it away,
Just say **amabo te**.

Tibi gratias ago means thank you very much,
Tibi gratias ago means thank you, thank you very much.
If your mom gives you a cookie, say before you eat it up,
Say **tibi gratias ago**.

Please excuse me is **ignosce mihi**, please excu-use me,
Please excuse me is **ignosce mihi**, please excu-use me.
If you bump into a little man and make him spill his tea,
Say **ignosce mihi**
!

Practice Your Latin

1. Practice writing the phrases by tracing the dots.

2. Color the pictures and match them to the Latin phrases that you should use for situations pictured below.

   a. **tibi gratias ago** b. **amabo te** c. **ignosce mihi**

3. In the box to the right, draw a picture of something for which you said "**tibi gratias ago**," today.

"**Tibi gratias ago**."

Show What You Know

Circle the correct English meaning for these Latin phrases.

1. **ignosce mihi**	please	thank you	excuse me
2. **amabo te**	please	thank you	excuse me
3. **tibi gratias ago**	please	thank you	excuse me

Review

Circle the correct English meaning for these Latin words.

1. **mensa**	table	chair	book
2. **mater**	brother	father	mother
3. **sedete**	listen	sit	stand

Master Your Words

Well, **discipuli**, you have learned eight commands and three new Latin phrases! It is time once again to make sure you have mastered all of these new Latin words. Can you give the correct English word for every Latin word below?

Chapter 10 Words

1. **sede** ____________________

   sedete ____________________

2. **surge** ____________________

   surgite ____________________

3. **scribe** ____________________

   scribite ____________________

4. **repete** ____________________

   repetite ____________________

Chapter 11 Words/Phrases

1. audi ____________________

   audite ____________________

2. tace ____________________

   tacete ____________________

3. aperi librum ____________________

   aperite libros ____________________

4. attole manum ____________________

   attolite manus ____________________

Chapter 12 Phrases

1. amabo te ____________________

2. tibi gratias ago ____________________

3. ignosce mihi ____________________

Master Your Songs

Classroom Commands Song [Audio Files 12-13(C)/42-43(E)]

Sede, **sedete** in your seat,
In your seat, in your seat.
Surge, **surgite** on your feet,
Stand up on your feet.

Scribe, **scribite** write so neat,
Write so neat, write so neat.
Repete, **repitite**
After me, repeat.

Tace, **tacete** – quiet please,
Quiet please, quiet please.
Audi, **audite** listen up,
Listen up to me.

Aperi librum – open the book,
Open the book, open the book.
Attole manum – raise your hand,
Raise it nice and high.

Manners Song [Audio File 14(C)/44(E)]

When you ask for anything you have to say **amabo te**,
When you ask for anything you have to say **amabo te**.
If you really want to have it, don't just take it away,
Just say **amabo te**.

Tibi gratias ago means thank you very much,
Tibi gratias ago means thank you, thank you very much.
If your mom gives you a cookie, say before you eat it up,
Say **tibi gratias ago**.

Please excuse me is **ignosce mihi**, please excu-use me,
Please excuse me is **ignosce mihi**, please excu-use me.
If you bump into a little man and make him spill his tea,
Say **ignosce mihi**!

Activities

1. What did the **magister** tell the **discipuli** to do? Circle the correct answer.

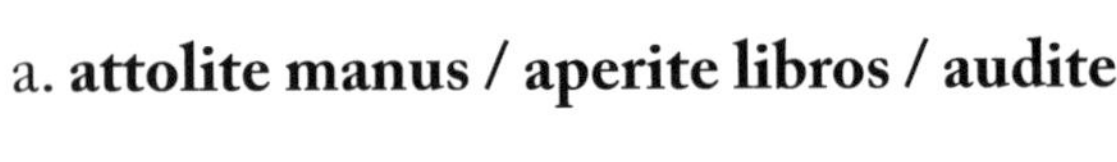

a. **attolite manus / aperite libros / audite**

b. **sedete / surgite / tacete**

c. **attolite manus / amabo te / surgite**

d. **sedete / audite / ignosce mihi**

e. **surge / tace / vale**

f. **amabo te / tace / audi**

g. **sede / scribe / surge**

2. What should these children say? Circle the correct answer:

a. 

ignosce mihi | **tibi gratias ago** | **surge**

b. 

audite | **ignosce mihi** | **tibi gratias ago**

c. 

aperi librum | **scribite** | **amabo te**

3. Play Simon Says! Listen as your teacher or a fellow student plays Simon and gives you commands. Remember you only have to obey when the leader first says, "Simon says…"

4. Have a pencil exchange! You will be giving pencils to three different people in your class. Here are the rules:

a. Greet each student in Latin.

b. Ask how they are in Latin.

c. Say **amabo te** for "please" when you request a pencil and **tibi gratias ago** for "thank you" when you are given a pencil.

Chapter Story

The Parable of the Vineyard

There was once a **vir**. Perhaps he was a **pater**. We do not know for sure. He had a large vineyard where grapes were grown. There were so many grapes in his vineyard that he needed help picking them, so early in the morning he went out to find some help. The first person he saw was a **puer**. "I see a **puer** to help me!" he shouted. He went quickly to the boy. "**Salve**!" he said. "**Quid agis**?"

The **puer** answered, "**Sum bene**."

The **vir** said, "**Surge** and come help me in my vineyard, **amabo te**! I will pay you well."

"I will," agreed the **puer**. "I have a **mater** and **frater** and **soror**, and I must provide money for them so that they may buy food. I will be happy to work for you."

And so the **puer** began to work hard picking grapes in the vineyard.

The owner of the vineyard, however, soon realized that he would need more help, so he went out again and looked until he saw a **vir** writing in a **liber** with his **stylus**. "**Salve**!" called the owner. "**Quid agis**?"

"**Sum pessime,**" said the **vir**. "I need money badly!"

"Then you are just the one I am looking for," said the owner. "Do not **sede**. Do not **scribe**. **Surge** and come! I need help picking grapes. I will pay you well."

"**Optime,**" said the **vir**. "I will be glad to work for you!"

And so the two of them worked and worked, but still there were grapes left on the vines.

Finally, the owner of the vineyard found one last **vir** who might help him. He was a lazy fellow. The owner tripped over him because he was lying down! "**Ignosce mihi**!" said the owner. "**Audi** me! I need help in my vineyard. I will pay you well. **Surge**!" The **vir** was lazy, but the owner of the vineyard was offering him a lot of money for only a little work, so he agreed.

The day was finally done, and all the grapes had been picked from the vines. One by one the workers came to the owner to receive their wages. He paid each one the same amount, no matter how long he had worked. The last man went away happy with his money, shouting "**Valete**!" over his shoulder as he went. The others, however, were not happy. The **puer** who had worked since the morning thought he deserved more money because he had worked longer than those who had come in the afternoon and night time. The **puer** and the **vir** with the **liber** complained, but the owner just said, "It is my money. You agreed to these wages, and I have the right to be generous with my money if I like. **Valete**!"

—*Adapted from Matthew 20: 1–16*

Chapter 14 Pets

Words to Learn

1. **canis** dog
2. **feles** cat
3. **equus** horse
4. **piscis** fish

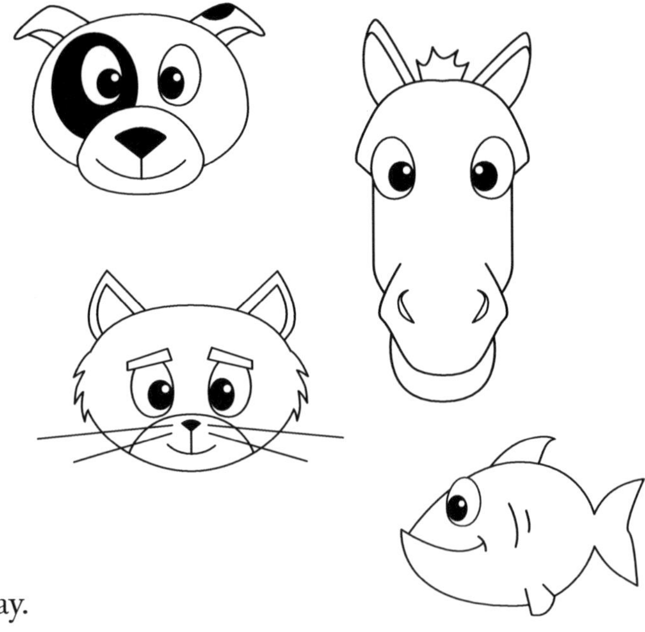

Chapter Song

Animal Song [Audio File 15(C)/45(E)]

Listen to the **canis** early in the morning,
Barking at the **feles** and makin' her run away.
"Meow" said the **feles** and went to catch a **piscis**,
And she climbed on an **equus** munching on his hay.
Neigh, neigh! Meow, meow! Off we go!

Chapter Lesson

Do you have any pets? If you do, you will probably learn its Latin name this week! Your new words are all animal names, and next week you will learn four more. Are animals things you can touch? Of course—just be careful about which ones you touch! That means these new Latin words are nouns. Do you remember that every Latin noun belongs to a family? There are five of these families, and they are called declensions. So, practice the animal words, and you can call everyone in your family by their Latin names, even your pets. Just don't call your dog a declension!

*__Apporta__ = Fetch

Practice Your Latin

1. Practice writing your new words by tracing the dots.

Canis Feles

Equus Piscis

2. Draw lines from the pictures to their Latin names.

equus

feles

canis

piscis

3. Fill in the blanks with the Latin word that fits best.

a. The **puer** threw a stick for his ________________ to fetch.

b. The **puella** put a saddle on her ________________ and rode him away.

c. The **vir** went to the pond with his fishing rod to catch a ________________.

d. The ______________ caught a big, fat mouse.

Show What You Know

Circle the correct English meaning for these Latin words.

1. **feles**	horse	fish	cat
2. **piscis**	dog	fish	horse
3. **canis**	dog	cat	fish
4. **equus**	fish	cat	horse

Review Words

Circle the correct English meaning for these Latin words.

1. **puella**	girl	boy	woman
2. **puer**	woman	girl	boy
3. **vir**	boy	man	woman
4. **femina**	man	girl	woman

Words to Learn

1. **leo** lion
2. **avis** bird
3. **ursa** bear
4. **elephantus** elephant

Chapter Song

Animal Song (Continued) [Audio File 16(C)/46(E)]

See the little **avis** flying 'round the **leo**,
"Roar" says the **leo** and scares away the bird.
Along comes the **ursa** and eats up all the honey,
Elephantus stomps around his little elephant herd.
Tweet, tweet! Roar, roar! Off we go!

Chapter Lesson

Last week you learned the word for dog—**canis**. Do you know that the Romans (who spoke Latin) used to warn people of mean dogs with signs just like we do? The way they said this in Latin was **cave canem** (beware of the dog!).

Famous Latin Saying

Each week from now on we will learn a famous Latin saying. Most of the sayings that you will learn are used by people who speak English. These Latin sayings are so famous that even people who speak English may know them!

This week work on memorizing **cave canem**—beware of the dog!

Practice Your Latin

1. Practice writing your new words by tracing the dots.

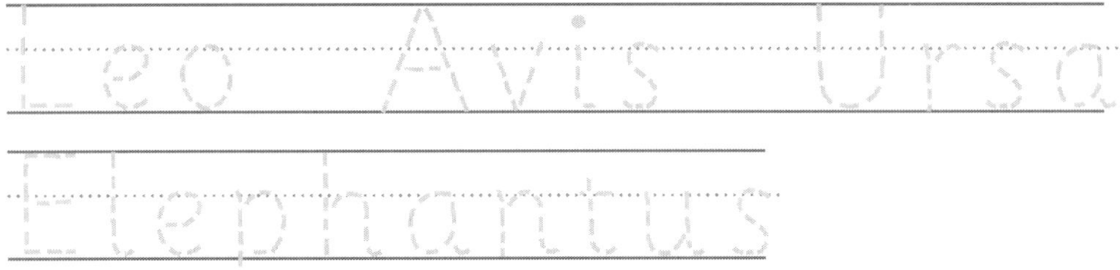

2. Draw pictures of a lion, bird, bear, and elephant above their Latin names.

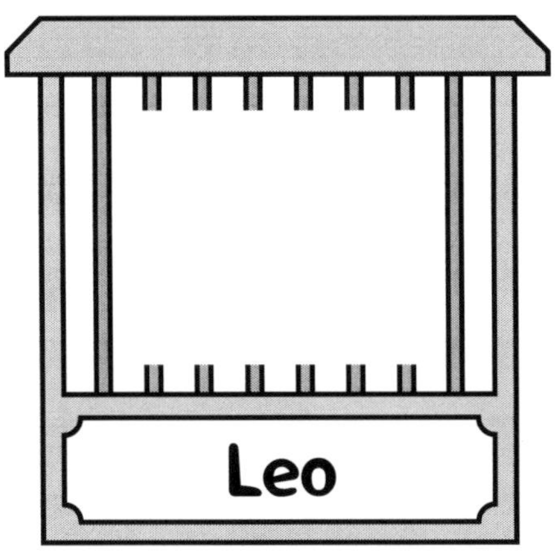

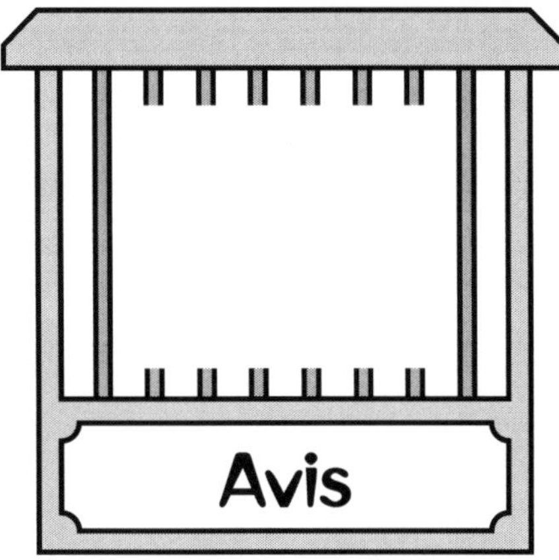

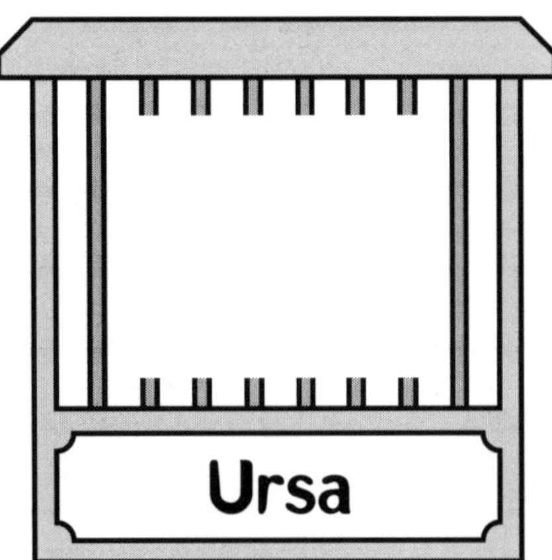

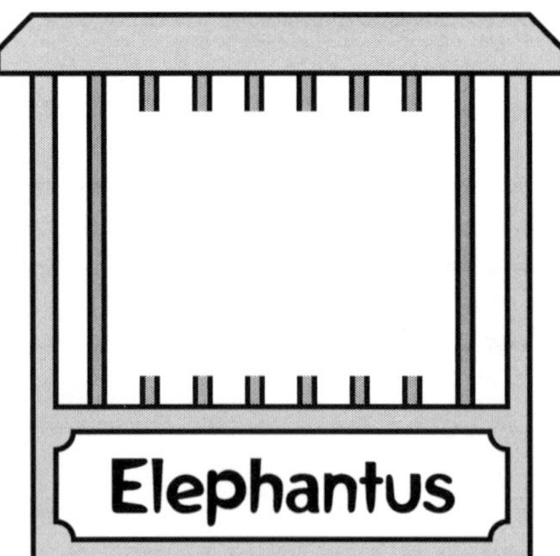

3. Match the Latin words to the English words.

a. **leo**	lion
b. **avis**	elephant
c. **ursa**	bird
d. **elephantus**	bear

Show What You Know

Circle the correct English meaning for these Latin words:

1. **elephantus**	bird	elephant	bear
2. **leo**	bear	elephant	lion
3. **ursa**	bear	bird	lion
4. **avis**	elephant	lion	bird

Review Words

Circle the correct English meaning for these Latin words:

1. **feles**	dog	bird	cat
2. **equus**	horse	fish	cat
3. **discipuli**	teacher	students	horse
4. **puer**	boy	cat	girl

Chapter 16

Christmas Words

Words to Learn

1. **angelus** angel
2. **pastor** shepherd
3. **agnus** lamb
4. **stella** star
5. **infans** baby

Chapter Song

Christmas Chant [Audio File 17(C)/47(E)]

Angelus – angel,
Stella – star,
Both appeared in the sky afar.

Pastor – shepherd,
Agnus – lamb,
Shepherds watching the little lambs.

Infans – baby,
Born in the hay,
Jesus, born on Christmas day.

Chapter Lesson

Christmas is coming soon and your new Latin words will help you remember the Christmas story. You also get to add one more animal name to your list—**agnus**! Did you notice that **stella** ends with an *a*? That means that it belongs to the first family of nouns, the first declension. **Infans** is another word that you can use all year. Is there an **infans** in your family? Have you ever had an **infans feles**?

Famous Latin Saying

This week your famous Latin saying is **rara avis**—"a rare bird." This phrase is not only used to describe a real **avis**, but also anything or anyone that is rare, unusual or interesting. You might call a friend who can throw a ball well with either hand a **rara avis**!

Grow Your English

Infans looks almost exactly like the English word "infant." That's because we borrowed it from Latin! It means the same thing in English as it does in Latin: a small baby.

Here is another English word that came from Latin: constellation. Constellation means a grouping of stars that make a shape in the sky. Have you ever seen the Big Dipper? That is part of a constellation known as Ursa Major. There are 88 known constellations, and they all have Latin names! Constellation is a long word, so the Latin is hard to find. If you look right in the middle of the word, though, you will see one of your new Latin words spelled out perfectly!

Practice Your Latin

1. Practice writing your new words by tracing the dots.

Angelus

Pastor Agnus

Stella Infans

2. Draw a line from the Latin words to the items in the picture.

angelus

pastor

stella

agnus

3. Fill in the sentences with the Latin word that fits best.

a. The ________________ was out in the field watching his flock.

b. The ________________ led the wise men to Bethlehem.

c. We were all born as a little ________________.

d. The ________________ appeared to the shepherds to tell them that a King was born.

e. The ________________ was asleep on the hillside.

4. Start practicing "Joy to the World" in Latin (found on page 63).

Show What You Know

Connect the English words to the Latin words.

1. **stella**	baby
2. **infans**	lamb
3. **pastor**	star
4. **agnus**	shepherd
5. **angelus**	angel

Review Words

Circle the English word that best matches the Latin word.

1. **ursa**	bear	bird	lion
2. **leo**	bear	bird	lion

Circle your answer.

3. Which Latin word did "infant" come from?

stella **pastor** **infans**

4. Which Latin word did "constellation" come from?

stella **mater** **agnus**

Chapter 17

More Christmas Words

Words to Learn

1. **cano** I sing
2. **laudo** I praise
3. **do** I give
4. **donum** gift

Chapter Song

<u>Christmas Chant (Continued)</u> [Audio File 18(C)/48(E)]

Cano – I sing,
On Christmas day,
Do a donum – in a cheerful way.

Donum – present,
Do – I give,
Laudo – every day I live.

Chapter Lesson

We have more words this week that make us think about Christmas. Look at your new words and ask yourself if they are things you can touch. **Donum** is a noun, because you can certainly touch a present. Three of your new words, though, are not nouns, because they are things you do. They are actions. Anything that you do is named by a verb. Verbs are words that describe actions. "I sing" is doing something, so it is a verb. What are the other two verbs?

These three verbs have the special ending on them that means "I." What is the letter on the end of each one? Yes – *o* is the special ending that means "I."

<u>Famous Latin Saying</u>

Vergil is a famous Roman writer who wrote a book called the *Aeneid* (ay-NEE-id). It features the hero Aeneas (ay-NEE-as) who travels from Troy to start the city of Rome. The first line of this famous book is **arma virumque cano**—"of arms and the man I sing." The man that Vergil will be singing or writing about is Aeneas!

Grow Your English

Do and **donum** give us the English word "donation." A donation is just a gift. It usually means a gift given for a special cause. Do you see the Latin hidden in the beginning of the word or the end of the word?

Practice Your Latin

1. Practice writing your new words by tracing the dots.

Cano Laudo

Do Donum

2. In the box below, draw a picture of a **donum** under a Christmas tree.

3. Fill in the sentences with the Latin word that fits best.

a. __________________ songs whenever I am happy.

b. __________________ presents to my friends.

c. I want to give a special __________________ to my mom.

d. __________________ the beautiful present I received.

4. Make a Christmas card and use Latin words. One way you can do this is to draw a Christmas picture and label the things that you know in Latin.

Show What You Know

Match the Latin words to the English words.

1. **do**	I sing
2. **donum**	gift
3. **cano**	I praise
4. **laudo**	I give

Review Words

Circle the English word that best matches the Latin word.

1. **stella**	star	shepherd	gift
2. **pastor**	star	shepherd	gift

Chapter 18 Review

Chapter 14 Words

1. **canis** ____________________

2. **feles** ____________________

3. **equus** ____________________

4. **piscis** ____________________

Chapter 15 Words

1. **leo** ____________________

2. **avis** ____________________

3. **ursa** ____________________

4. **elephantus** ____________________

Chapter 16 Words

1. **angelus** ____________________

2. **pastor** ____________________

3. **agnus** ____________________

4. **stella** ____________________

5. **infans** ____________________

Chapter 17 Words

1. **do** ____________________

2. **donum** ____________________

3. **cano** ____________________

4. **laudo** ____________________

Master Your Songs

Animal Song [Audio Files 15-16(C)/45-46(E)]

Listen to the **canis** early in the morning,
Barking at the **feles** and makin' her run away.
"Meow" said the **feles** and went to catch a **piscis**,
And she climbed on an **equus** munching on his hay.
Neigh, neigh! Meow, meow! Off we go!

See the little **avis** flying 'round the **leo**,
"Roar" says the **leo** and scares away the bird.
Along comes the **ursa** and eats up all the honey,
Elephantus stomps around his little elephant herd.
Tweet, tweet! Roar, roar! Off we go!

Christmas Chant [Audio Files 17-18(C)/47-48(E)]

Angelus – angel,
Stella – star,
Both appeared in the sky afar.

Pastor – shepherd,
Agnus – lamb,
Shepherds watching the little lambs.

Infans – baby,
Born in the hay,
Jesus, born on Christmas day.

Cano – I sing,
On Christmas day,
Do a donum – in a cheerful way.

Donum – present,
Do – I give,
Laudo – every day I live.

Joy to the World *(Here is an additional song for you to pratice.)*
Laetissimus, Accipiat, Iam mundus Dominum.
Dum omnia in corda nos,
Accipimus illum,
Accipimus illum,
Accip-, accipimus, illum.

Activities

1. Circle your answers.

a. Which animal can fly?

elephantus **avis** **leo**

b. Which of these animals is the heaviest?

canis **feles** **elephantus**

c. Which one of these animals lives in the water?

piscis **ursa** **equus**

d. Which one of these animals does a cowboy ride?

feles **equus** **leo**

e. What do you get on your birthday?

elephantus **donum** **ursa**

f. If you are in a choir, what do you do?

cano **canis** **do**

g. Who watches the sheep in the field?

do **pastor** **infans**

h. Who came to tell the shepherds about the birth of Jesus?

ursa **equus** **angelus**

i. Jesus came to earth as a tiny _____.

infans **cano** **angelus**

2. Put all of the animals back in their proper places! Color each animal and draw a line to their proper cage.

Chapter Story

<u>Christmas Announcement</u>

On a cold night, long ago, there were **pastores** out on a hillside watching their **agnos**. It was quiet and dark, and the **agni** were asleep. All of a sudden, an **angelus** appeared in the sky with a host of other **angeli**. The **pastores** were very afraid! But the **angelus** said, "Don't be afraid! I have wonderful news!" And the **angelus** told them that Jesus the Savior was born that night and told them that they would find the **infans** Jesus in a barn, sleeping in a manger.

Then many **angeli** appeared with him and sang "Glory to God!" The **pastores** were so excited that they left the **agnos** and went to find the **infans** Jesus. They found him in a barn, with Mary and Joseph, as the **angelus** said. Each shepherd bowed down in worship and praise.

Later, the Wise Men came to see the **infans** Jesus, too. They saw a bright **stella** in the sky. They followed the **stella** to Jesus, and they each brought a precious **donum** to him. "**Donum Iesu do,**" said the first wise man as he gave gold to Jesus. The second wise man gave Jesus frankincense and the third gave him myrrh.

Chapter 19 The Body

Words to Learn

1. **manus** hand
2. **pes** foot
3. **caput** head
4. **corpus** body

Chapter Song

<u>Action Song</u> [Audio File 19(C)/49(E)]

If you're happy and you know it, wave your hand – **man-us**!
If you're happy and you know it, wave your hand – **man-us**!
If you're happy and you know it, then your face will surely show it,
If you're happy and you know it, wave your hand – **man-us**!

If you're happy and you know it, stomp your foot – **pes**, **pes**!
If you're happy and you know it, stomp your foot – **pes**, **pes**!
If you're happy and you know it, then your face will surely show it,
If you're happy and you know it, stomp your foot – **pes**, **pes**!

If you're happy and you know it, nod your head – **ca-put**!
If you're happy and you know it, nod your head – **ca-put**!
If you're happy and you know it, then your face will surely show it,
If you're happy and you know it, nod your head – **ca-put**!

If you're happy and you know it, spin around – **cor-pus**!
If you're happy and you know it, spin around – **cor-pus**!
If you're happy and you know it, then your face will surely show it,
If you're happy and you know it, spin around – **cor-pus**!

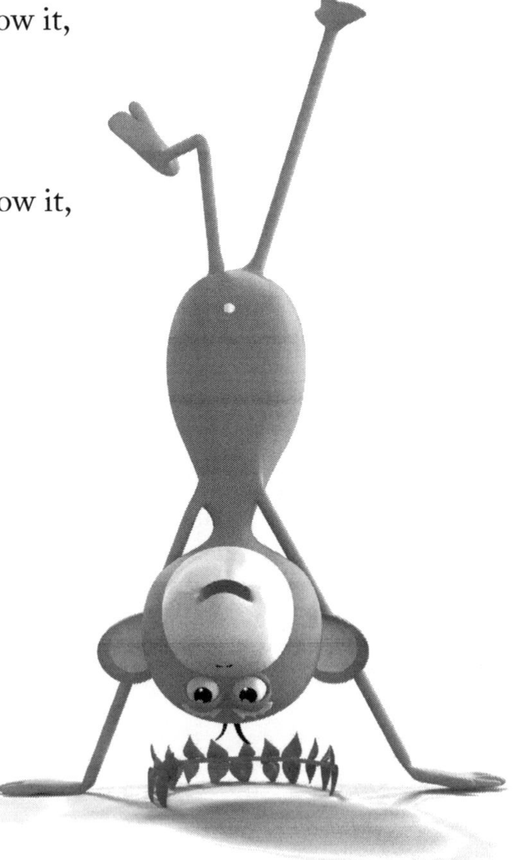

Chapter Lesson

Isn't your body (**corpus**) wonderfully put together? Think of all the things that you can do with the parts of your **corpus** that you are learning in Latin this week. You can draw with your **manus**, or hop on your **pes**. Try to use your new words often. It's really fun to walk up to your friend and say, "There's an **avis** on your **caput**!" or, "Let me shake your **manus**!" See how many times you can use your new words in conversation this week.

Famous Latin Saying

In a country where the people can vote, they can have a "voice" in deciding who will be the leader or president. Once a president has been elected, we can say that the **vox populi**, "the voice of the people," has been heard.

Grow Your English

There are many English words that come from the Latin words for hand and foot. "Manuscript" means "written by hand." "Manual" means that you have to do it "by hand." You can guess which Latin word they came from! A "pedestrian" is someone who is "on foot." If you are riding on a bike or in a car, you are not a pedestrian. Whenever you are walking on your feet, though, you are. You can see the Latin word for foot right in the beginning of the word.

Practice Your Latin

1. Practice writing your new words by tracing the dots.

Manus Pes

Caput Corpus

2. Using the picture to the right, follow the instrustions below.

a. Draw a hat on the boy's **caput**.

b. Draw boots on the boy's **pes**.

c. Draw a coat on the boy's **corpus**.

d. Draw gloves on the boy's **manus**.

3. Circle your answer to complete each sentence.

a. Kick the ball with your:

manus	**corpus**	**leo**	**pes**

b. Put your hat on your:

pes	**corpus**	**agnus**	**caput**

c. Please raise your _________ before you speak!

caput	**stella**	**manus**	**pes**

d. My whole _________ has many parts!

manus	**pes**	**corpus**	**caput**

Show What You Know

Match the Latin words to their English meanings.

1. **manus**	foot
2. **corpus**	hand
3. **pes**	head
4. **caput**	body

Review

Match the Latin words to their English meanings.

1. **liber**	pencil
2. **agnus**	baby
3. **stylus**	book
4. **infans**	lamb

Chapter 20 The Face

Words to Learn

1. **auris** ear
2. **nares** nose
3. **oculus** eye
4. **os** mouth

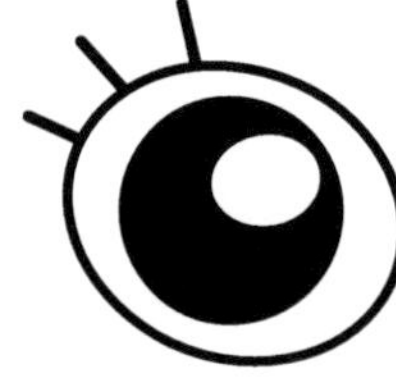

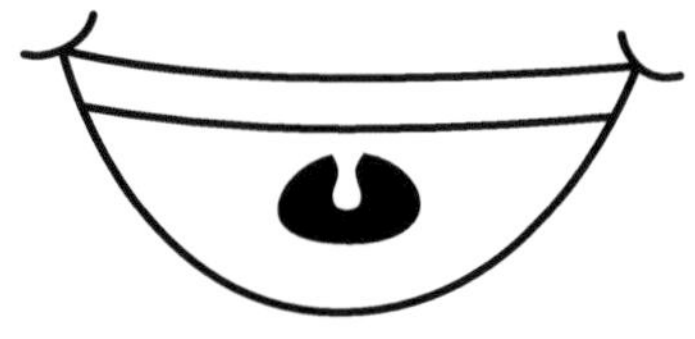

Chapter Song

<u>Action Song (Continued)</u> [Audio File 20(C)/50(E)]

If you're happy and you know it, touch your nose – **na-res**!
If you're happy and you know it, touch your nose – **na-res**!
If you're happy and you know it, then your face will surely show it,
If you're happy and you know it, touch your nose – **na-res**!

If you're happy and you know it, tug your ear – **au-ris**!
If you're happy and you know it, tug your ear – **au-ris**!
If you're happy and you know it, then your face will surely show it,
If you're happy and you know it, tug your ear – **au-ris**!

If you're happy and you know it, wink your eye – **oculus**!
If you're happy and you know it, wink your eye – **oculus**!
If you're happy and you know it, then your face will surely show it,
If you're happy and you know it, wink your eye – **oculus**!

If you're happy and you know it, close your mouth – **os, os**! (finger to lips)
If you're happy and you know it, close your mouth – **os, os**!
If you're happy and you know it, then your face will surely show it,
If you're happy and you know it, close your mouth – **os, os**!

Chapter Lesson

The new words in this chapter are naming the parts of you that help you discover and explore things around you. Your **oculus** allows you to see things. Your **nares** allows you to smell things. Your **auris** allows you to hear things, and your **os** allows you to taste things, as well as speak. These are called your "senses." These parts of you also allow you to make all kinds of interesting expressions! Wrinkle your **nares** and open your **os** wide.

Famous Latin Saying

Look at the words **vox populi**. Can you see how easily our English word "voice" comes from **vox**? We also get our word "vocal" from **vox**. Do you know what your vocal cords are? Can you see that our word "people" comes from **populi**? We also get our word "population" from **populi**.

Grow Your English

Binoculars. There really is a Latin word in there that you know! Binoculars are like extra power for your eyes so that you can see things far away. You look through binoculars with your eyes. Look at the part of the word after "bin" and you can see part of the Latin word for "eye."

Practice Your Latin

1. Practice writing your new words by tracing the dots.

Auris Nares

Oculus Os

2. Make lunch bag puppets and glue on the facial features labeled in Latin.

3. Play "Simon Says!" using vocabulary from Chapters 19 to 20.

4. Match the questions to your answers.

a. What do you use to smell?	**auris**
b. What do you use to see?	**os**
c. What do you use to hear?	**nares**
d. What do you use to taste?	**oculus**

Show What You Know

Match the Latin words to their English meanings.

1. **nares**	mouth
2. **oculus**	nose
3. **auris**	eye
4. **os**	ear

Review

Match the Latin words to their English meanings.

1. **mensa**	house
2. **sella**	wall
3. **casa**	table
4. **murus**	chair

Words to Learn

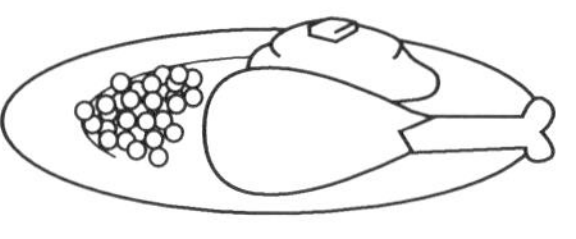

1. **cibus** food
2. **aqua** water
3. **cena** dinner
4. **edo** I eat
5. **bibo** I drink

Chapter Song

Edo Song [Audio File 21(C)/51(E)]

Edo my **cibus** when it's time to eat!
Edo my **cibus** when it's time to eat!
Because I love the good food my mother makes! **Cibus**! **Cibus**!

Bibo my **aqua** when I play hard!
Bibo my **aqua** when I play hard!
When I'm thirsty, **bibo** right away! **Bibo**! **Bibo**!

It's time for **cena**, gather everyone!
It's time for **cena**, gather everyone!
We're ready to eat our **cena** tonight! **Cena**! **Cena**!

Chapter Lesson

This week, you get to learn words about food and eating! There are a lot of ways you can use these words every day. Be careful not to confuse **cibus** and **cena**. They look and sound similar. There are nouns and verbs in your new word list. Can you tell which ones are verbs? Remember that verbs are action words, things that you do. How many nouns are there?

<u>Famous Latin Saying</u>

You will hear people say "**et cetera**" (meaning "and others") a lot. It is one of those Latin phrases that is used a lot in English. In writing, it abbreviated as "etc." You can use this phrase whenever you want to say "and others" or "and other things." For example, you could say, "At the picnic, we served hot dogs, hamburgers, watermelon, pies, cakes, et cetera."

Grow Your English

Have you ever visited a big aquarium? Do you have a little aquarium in your home? An aquarium is a place where people keep fish and other sea creatures. They hold water, because fish need water to live. Look at the first half of the word "aquarium" and find the Latin word in it!

Practice Your Latin

1. Practice writing your new words by tracing the dots.

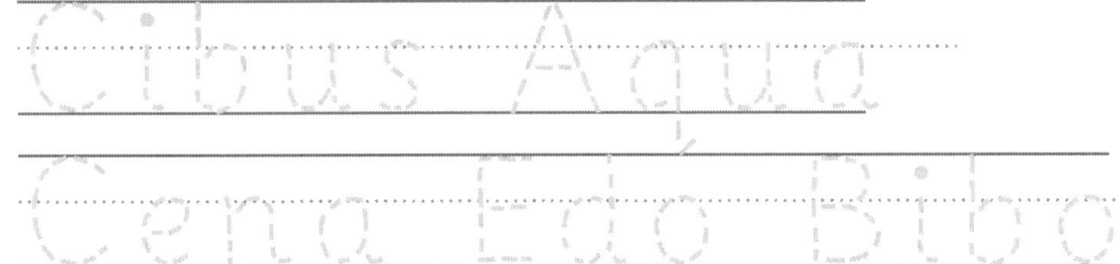

2. Draw a line from these Latin words to the matching picture.

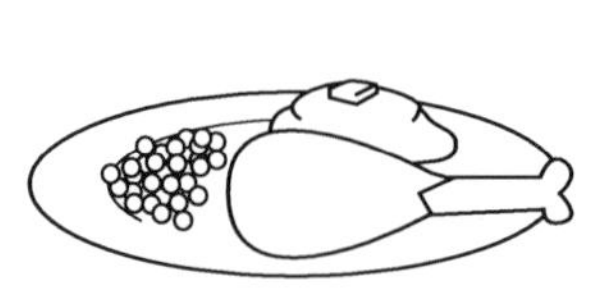

edo

bibo

cibus

aqua

3. Read or listen to the sentence and circle your answer.

a. ___________ french fries when we go out to eat.	**edo**	**bibo**	**cena**
b. We eat ___________ at six o'clock.	**aqua**	**cibus**	**cena**
c. My favorite ___________ is cookies.	**bibo**	**cibus**	**aqua**
d. Drink a lot of ___________ every day!	**cena**	**edo**	**aqua**
e. ___________ orange juice in the morning.	**bibo**	**cena**	**cibus**

Show What You Know

Match the Latin words to the English meaning.

1. **bibo**	water
2. **edo**	food
3. **cibus**	dinner
4. **aqua**	I drink
5. **cena**	I eat

Review

Match the Latin words to the English meaning.

1. **Meum praenomen est**	good-bye
2. **Quid est tuum praenomen?**	My name is
3. **salve**	What is your name?
4. **vale**	hello

Chapter 22

More Food Words

Words to Learn

1. **panis** bread
2. **fructus** fruit
3. **lac** milk
4. **crustulum** cookie
5. **pullus** chicken

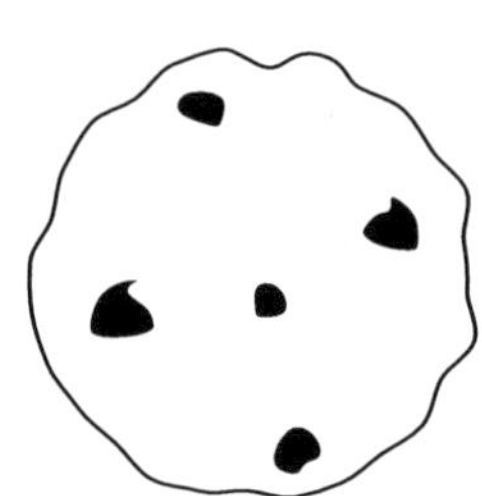

Chapter Song

Cibus Chant [Audio File 22(C)/52(E)]

Panis—bread. (clap-clap-clap)
Panis—bread. (clap-clap-clap)

Fructus—fruit. (stomp-stomp-stomp)
Fructus—fruit. (stomp-stomp-stomp)

Lac—milk. (clap-clap-clap)
Lac—milk. (clap-clap-clap)

Crustulum—cookie. (stomp-stomp-stomp)
Crustulum—cookie. (stomp-stomp-stomp)

Pullus—chicken. (clap-clap)
Pullus—chicken. (clap-clap)

Chapter Lesson

Last week you learned words about eating; this week you are learning the words for five things that you eat. You drink **lac**, though, of course! Which one in the list is your favorite? You might eat your **pullus** in little nuggets, but **pullus** is also what you call a chicken that is alive. So, you can add one more animal word to your list! What is your favorite kind of **crustulum**? Do you have any **panis** in your lunchbox or pantry? Is a banana a **fructus** or a **crustulum**?

<u>Famous Latin Saying</u>

Can you create a sentence in which you use the phrase **et cetera**? Remember, you can abbreviate **et cetera** by simply writing "etc." Here is an example: "For dinner we will have **pullus, panis, fructus, crustulum,** etc." This sentence would mean: "For dinner we will have chicken, bread, fruit, a cookie, and other things."

Grow Your English

The pantry is where you keep food, or "your daily bread." Look at the beginning of the word; can you guess which Latin word it came from?

Practice Your Latin

1. Practice writing your new words by tracing the dots.

Panis Fructus Lac

Crustulum Pullus

2. Circle your answer.

a. Would you find chocolate chips in a **crustulum** or **pullus**?

crustulum **pullus**

b. Do you drink **lac** or **panis** with your **crustulum**?

lac **panis**

c. Do you make a peanut butter and jelly sandwich with **pullus** or **panis**?

pullus **panis**

d. Do you barbecue **lac** or **pullus**?

lac **pullus**

e. Are apples **fructus** or **panis**?

fructus **panis**

3. Cut out and color the food shapes. Label them with the right Latin words! When your teacher calls out the Latin words, hold up the right picture! Save your cutouts for other games. (See page 123 for larger cutouts.)

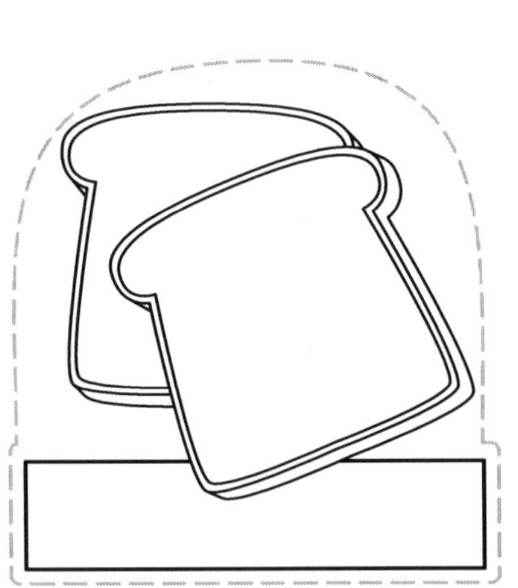

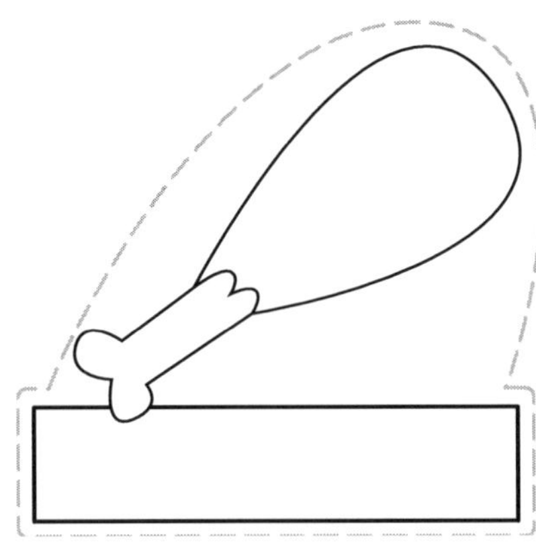

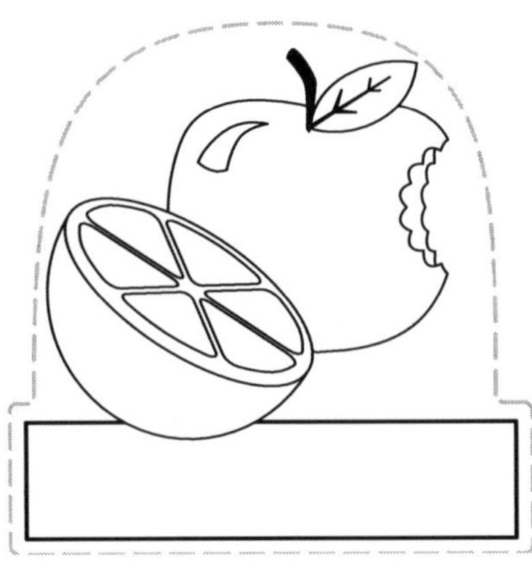

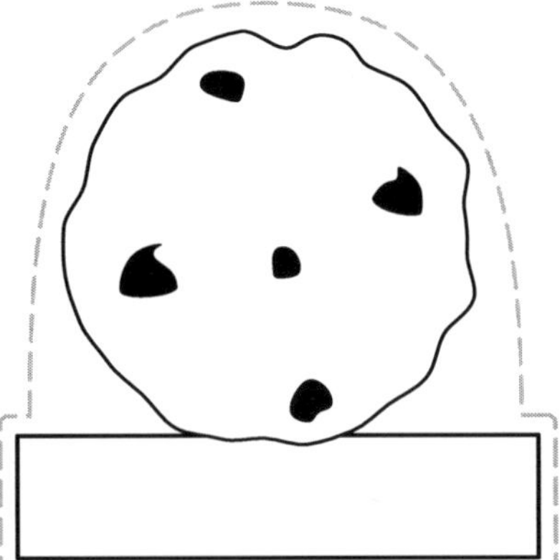

4. In the box below draw a picture of your favorite kind of **crustulum**.

Crustulum

Show What You Know

Match the Latin words to the English meaning.

1. **lac**	bread
2. **fructus**	milk
3. **crustulum**	chicken
4. **pullus**	cookie
5. **panis**	fruit

Review

Circle the English word or phrase that best matches the Latin.

1. **amabo te**	please	thank you
2. **tibi gratias ago**	please	thank you

Chapter 23 Review

Chapter 19 Words

1. **manus** ____________________

2. **pes** ____________________

3. **caput** ____________________

4. **corpus** ____________________

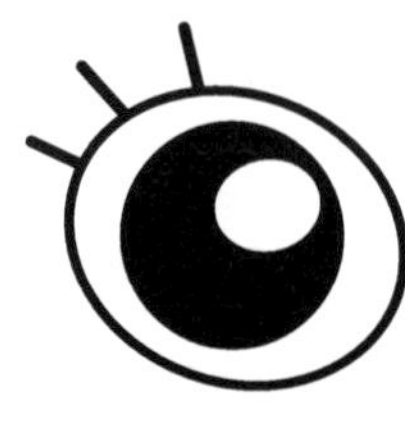

Chapter 20 Words

1. **auris** ____________________

2. **nares** ____________________

3. **oculus** ____________________

4. **os** ____________________

Chapter 21 Words

1. **cibus** ____________________

2. **aqua** ____________________

3. **cena** ____________________

4. **edo** ____________________

5. **bibo** ____________________

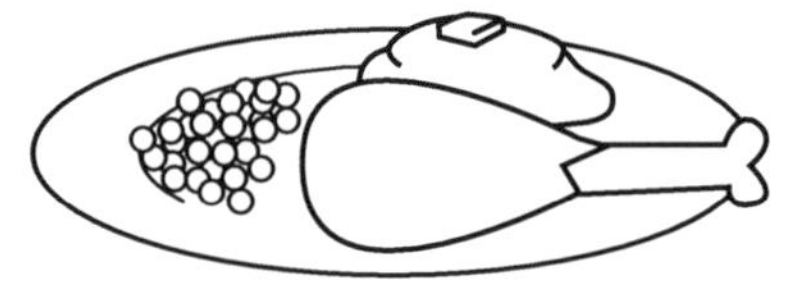

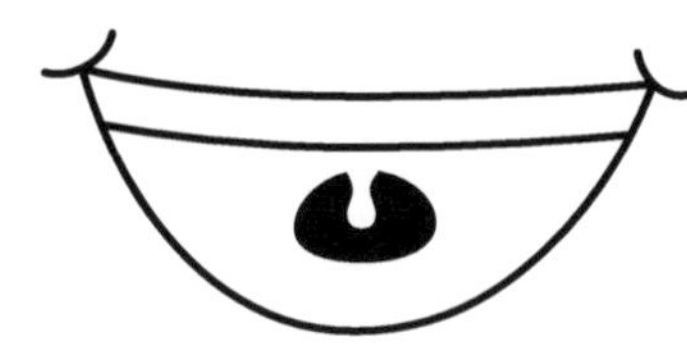

Chapter 22 Words

1. **panis** ______________________

2. **fructus** ______________________

3. **lac** ______________________

4. **crustulum** ______________________

5. **pullus** ______________________

Master Your Songs

<u>Action Song</u> [Audio Files 19-20(C)/49-50(E)]
Here is a condensed version. Watch your teacher's motions carefully so you will know what the next line is.

If you're happy and you know it, wave your hand – **man-us**!
If you're happy and you know it, stomp your foot – **pes**, **pes**!
If you're happy and you know it, then your face will surely show it,
If you're happy and you know it, nod your head – **ca-put**!

If you're happy and you know it, spin around – **cor-pus**!
If you're happy and you know it, touch your nose – **na-res**!
If you're happy and you know it, then your face will surely show it,
If you're happy and you know it, tug your ear – **au-ris**!

If you're happy and you know it, wink your eye – **oculus**!
If you're happy and you know it, close your mouth – **os**, **os**!
If you're happy and you know it, then your face will surely show it,
If you're happy and you know it, wave your hand – **man-us**!

<u>Edo Song</u> [Audio File 21(C)/51(E)]

Edo my **cibus** when it's time to eat!
Edo my **cibus** when it's time to eat!
Because I love the good food that my mother makes! **Cibus**! **Cibus**!

Bibo my **aqua** when I play hard!
Bibo my **aqua** when I play hard!
When I'm thirsty, **bibo** right away! **Bibo**! **Bibo**!

It's time for **cena**, gather everyone!
It's time for **cena**, gather everyone!
We're ready to eat our **cena** tonight! **Cena**! **Cena**!

Cibus Chant [Audio File 22(C)/52(E)]

Here is a silly chant about food that you can sing or just listen to. Listen for the Latin words!

Panis—bread. (clap-clap-clap)
Panis—bread. (clap-clap-clap)

Fructus—fruit. (stomp-stomp-stomp)
Fructus—fruit. (stomp-stomp-stomp)

Lac—milk. (clap-clap-clap)
Lac—milk. (clap-clap-clap)

Crustulum—cookie. (stomp-stomp-stomp)
Crustulum—cookie. (stomp-stomp-stomp)

Pullus—chicken. (clap-clap)
Pullus—chicken. (clap-clap)

Canis Song [Audio File 23(C)/53(E)]

There once was a **canis** who loved to eat bread.
He liked to speak Latin and stand on his head.
He learned to say "**panis**" and "**amabo te**."
If you say the same you can eat bread today.
Say, **panis, amabo te,** please pass the bread.

This **canis**, he also loved cookies with milk;
The other dogs didn't like dogs of his ilk.
But if he had **lac** and a big **crustulum**,
He didn't much care who hung out in his room.
Say, **lac** and a **crustulum**, cookies and milk.

They served him his dinner of chicken and fruit,
He picked up his trumpet and started to toot.
It turns out he doesn't like **pullus** at all,
And he thought that the **fructus** was his rubber ball.
Say, **pullus** is chicken and **fructus** is fruit.

Activities

1. Play "Simon Says" using words from this review chapter.

2. In the box to the right, draw a picture of yourself and draw a line from each Latin word to that part of you.

manus

pes

caput

nares

os

oculus

auris

3. Fill in the matching Latin words for the sentences below, choosing from this list: **oculus, auris, os, nares**.

This horse has a big ____________!

This cat is twitching her ____________!

This bear is winking his ____________!

4. What is your favorite kind of **fructus**?
Draw a picture of it on the plate.

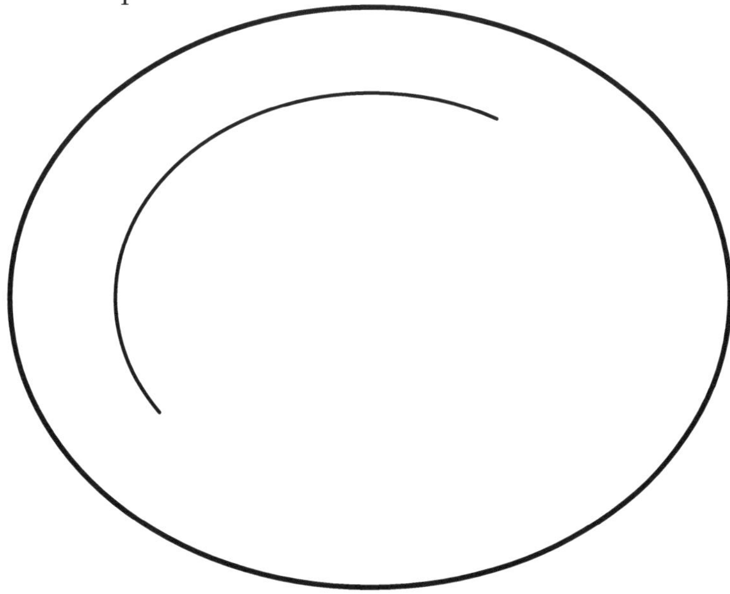

5. It's time to make Silly Sandwiches! Take out your food cutouts from Chapter 22 and put them on the table in front of you. Listen carefully to your teacher's instructions. When she asks you to find a specific food, take it and put it on your "sandwich". When she says: "**surgite**," stand up and wait for your teacher to check to make sure that you have all the parts of your "sandwich" in the correct order. If you do, you may "eat" your sandwich. If they are not in the correct order, you must put them back in the pile and start over. Whoever has "eaten" all of their food pieces first wins.

6. Your mother wrote her shopping list in Latin! Draw a line from the pictures to each item on the list.

Chapter Story

Follow along as your teacher reads, and circle the best answer for each blank.

Cena Time!

"It's almost time for **canis / cena**!" said **Mater**. "Help me set the **mensa / nares, amabo te**. Wash up first." The **equus / puella** quickly washed up and helped her **mater**. **Mater** put the **cibus / feles** on the **mensa / murus** and said, "Call your **pater** and **frater** for **cena**!" **Pater** and **frater** washed up and then sat down in their **sella / fenestra**. "Pass the **pullus / puer, amabo te**," he said. **Frater** said, "**Edo** my **panis / auris** first!" The **puella** said "**Bibo** my **lac / fructus** first, but I will save some for my **feles / stylus** to drink." **Frater** took another piece of **edo / panis**. "Close your **os / caput** when you eat, **amabo te**!" said **Mater**. "When you clean up your plates, we will have a **aqua / crustulum** for dessert." "Yum!" said the **puella**, "**Edo** my **pullus / pes** quickly!" When they finished eating, everyone helped to clear the dishes and the **fenestra / cibus** off of the table. "**Tibi gratias ago** for making a good **cena / nares**!" said **Pater**.

Words to Learn

1. **nix** snow
2. **imber** rain
3. **ventus** wind
4. **nimbus** cloud
5. **arcus** rainbow

Chapter Song

Weather Song [Audio File 24(C)/54(E)]

In the springtime,
When the rain comes,
Use your umbrella in the **imber**.
When the **ventus** blows,
And it's nipping at your nose,
Come inside out of the weather.

After rainstorms,
After **imber**,
Sometimes you see a pretty rainbow.
If you look up high,
There's an **arcus** in the sky,
The whole earth is glowing with a rainbow.

In the winter,
When the snow comes,
Nix covers everything in sight.
And the clouds are gray,
Every **nimbus** comes to play,
A **nix-nimbus** makes the world white.

Chapter Lesson

This week you will learn words about the weather. They are all nouns. Do you get much **nix** where you live? Name some of the fun things you can do in the **nix**. Have you ever seen a double **arcus**? Do you ever see shapes in a **nimbus**? Which one of your new Latin words best describes the weather today?

<u>Famous Latin Saying</u>

Festina lente, "make haste slowly," is a good phrase for students to learn well. It means that the best way to speed ahead is often to go slowly. In other words you will get work done fastest if you take your time and do it correctly so you don't have to do it again! Have you ever tried to do something too fast and then made a mistake so that you had to start all over again?

Practice Your Latin

1. Practice writing your new words by tracing the dots.

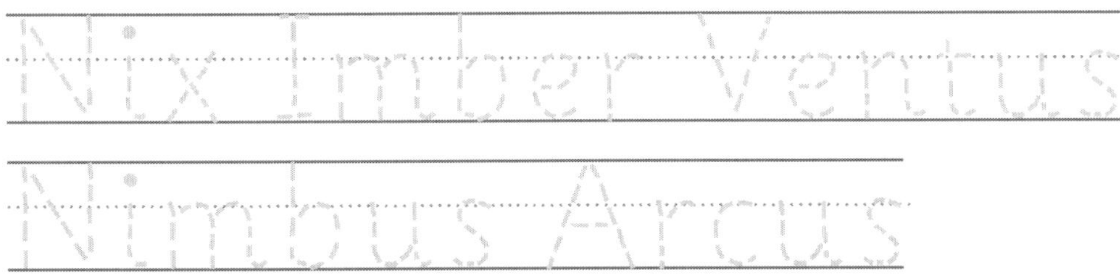

2. Using the pictures below, follow these instructions: a) Draw the things on the **puer** that he might need to go out in the **imber**; b) Draw the things on the **puella** that she might need to go out in the **nix**.

* 4. Color and cut out the rain, snowflake, rainbow, cloud, and wind and label them with the Latin names. Hold up the right shape when your teacher calls out the Latin words!

Show What You Know

Match the Latin words to English words.

1. **nix**	cloud
2. **imber**	snow
3. **arcus**	wind
4. **nimbus**	rainbow
5. **ventus**	rain

Review

Match the Latin words to English words.

1. **mensa**	book
2. **liber**	write
3. **sede**	rise/stand up
4. **surge**	table
5. **scribe**	sit down

Chapter 25 The Seasons

Words to Learn

1. **hiems** winter
2. **ver** spring
3. **autumnus** fall
4. **aestas** summer

Chapter Song

Seasons Song [Audio File 25(C)/55(E)]

A gust of fall wind, blowing leaves,
Tells me that **autumnus** is here.
The white **nix** covers each blade of grass,
And I know that the **hiems** is drawing near.

The spring flowers bloom and grass turns green,
I see that the **ver** is on its way.
The sun beats down on the summer fields,
For the **aestas** has come with a sunny day.

Chapter Lesson

Last week you learned words about the weather. Weather changes with the seasons in most places. This week you will learn the Latin words for the four seasons. Do you have a favorite season? There is something special and beautiful about each one.

Famous Latin Saying

Festina Lente ("make haste slowly." **Festina** means "make haste" and **lente** means "slowly.") You will "make haste" or go quickly when you slow down enough to do something correctly. The famous American named Benjamin Franklin once said that "Haste makes waste." This week try not to go so fast that you make needless mistakes that end up taking up even more of your time!

Grow Your English

Autumnus looks very much like autumn, doesn't it? You have probably heard that word; "autumn" is another English word for "fall." Can you guess where we got it from?

Practice Your Latin

1. Practice writing your new words by tracing the dots.

Hiems Ver

Autumnus Aestas

2. In which season do you usually use or see these items? Connect each of these items listed on the left and right to the seasons listed in the middle. Answers may vary.

3. Circle a Latin word to complete each sentence.

a. I like to go sledding in the ________.

hiems **ver** **autumnus** **aestas**

b. I rake leaves in the ___________.

hiems **ver** **autumnus** **aestas**

c. ______ is the best time for swimming.

hiems **ver** **autumnus** **aestas**

d. Flowers start blooming in the _______.

hiems **ver** **autumnus** **aestas**

e. Leaves turn pretty colors in the _____.

hiems **ver** **autumnus** **aestas**

f. Christmas comes in the _________.

hiems **ver** **autumnus** **aestas**

4. Draw a picture of your favorite thing to do in each season. If you like to swim in the summer, you could draw a pool; if you like to sled in the winter, you could draw a sled. Use your imagination!

Ver	**Aestas**
Autumnus	**Hiems**

Show What You Know

Circle the Latin word that best matches the English word.

1. winter	**hiems**	**ver**	**autumnus**	**aestas**
2. spring	**hiems**	**ver**	**autumnus**	**aestas**
3. fall	**hiems**	**ver**	**autumnus**	**aestas**
4. summer	**hiems**	**ver**	**autumnus**	**aestas**

Review

Circle the English word or phrase that best matches the Latin.

1. **Quid agis?**	hello	well/fine	How are you?
2. **bene**	great	well/fine	terrible
3. **optime**	terrible	good-bye	great

Chapter 26
The Sky

Words to Learn

1. **caelum** sky
2. **luna** moon
3. **stella** star
4. **sol** sun

Chapter Song

<u>Caelum Song</u> [Audio File 26(C)/56(E)]

Luna moon and **stella** star,
How I wonder what you are.
Up above in the **caelum** high,
Like a diamond in the sky.
When the nighttime turns to day,
Then the **sol** comes out to stay.

Chapter Lesson

This week you will learn four words about the sky. One of them you already know – **stella**! This should be an easy chapter to master. Try to go out and look at the **luna** and **stellas** up in the **caelum** this week!

Famous Latin Saying

E pluribus unum—"out of many, one." This is the motto on the Great Seal of the United States. People came out of many different nations to form one new nation—The United States. The words **e pluribus** mean "out of many" (many nations or peoples). The word **unum** means "one." Though there are many stars, there is only one…**caelum**.

Grow Your English

A lunar shuttle goes to the moon on a lunar mission. "Lunar" comes from one of your new Latin words. Which one does it sound like?

Practice Your Latin

1. Practice writing your new words by tracing the dots.

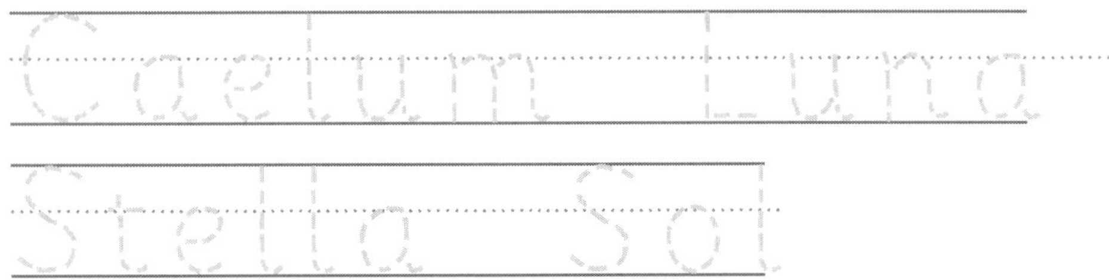

2. Cut out and color the **luna**, **sol**, **nimbus**, and **stellas**. Label them each with the right Latin words. Turn to page 129 and paste them to the matching **caelum**. (See page 125 for larger cutouts.)

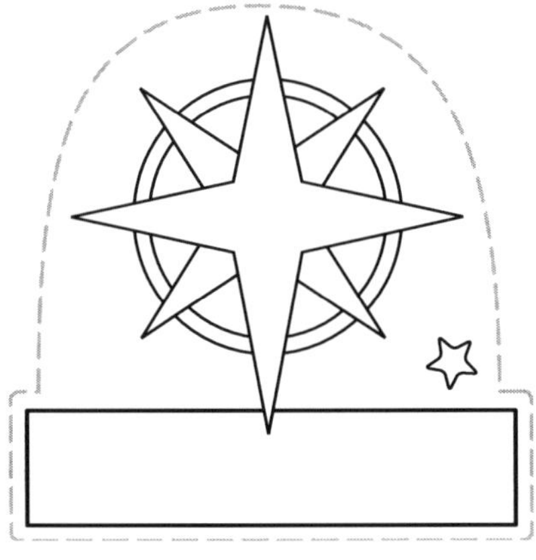

3. Circle your answer to complete the sentence.

a. The ________ shines when it is day.	**luna**	**sol**	**caelum**
b. The cow jumped over the ________!	**luna**	**stella**	**sol**
c. I saw a falling ________ in the sky.	**caelum**	**stella**	**sol**
d. The airplane took off into the ________.	**luna**	**stella**	**caelum**

Show What You Know

Match the Latin word to the English word.

1. **luna**	sky
2. **sol**	star
3. **stella**	moon
4. **caelum**	sun

Review

Match the Latin word or phrase to the English.

1. **attole manum**	please
2. **audi**	be quiet
3. **amabo te**	listen
4. **tace**	excuse me
5. **ignosce mihi**	raise your hand

Chapter 27

Review

Chapter 24 Words

1. **nix** ______________________
2. **imber** ______________________
3. **ventus** ______________________
4. **nimbus** ______________________
5. **arcus** ______________________

Chapter 25 Words

1. **hiems** ______________________
2. **ver** ______________________
3. **autumnus** ______________________
4. **aestas** ______________________

Chapter 26 Words

1. **caelum** ______________________
2. **luna** ______________________
3. **stella** ______________________
4. **sol** ______________________

Master Your Songs

<u>Weather Song</u> [Audio File 24(C)/54(E)]

In the springtime,
When the rain comes,
Use your umbrella in the **imber**.
When the **ventus** blows,
And it's nipping at your nose,
Come inside out of the weather.

After rainstorms,
After **imber**,
Sometimes you see a pretty rainbow.
If you look up high,
There's an **arcus** in the sky,
The whole earth is glowing with a rainbow.

In the winter,
When the snow comes,
Nix covers everything in sight.
And the clouds are gray,
Every **nimbus** comes to play,
A **nix-nimbus** makes the world white.

<u>Seasons Song</u> [Audio File 25(C)/55(E)]

A gust of fall wind, blowing leaves,
Tells me that **autumnus** is here.
The white **nix** covers each blade of grass,
And I know that the **hiems** is drawing near.

The spring flowers bloom and grass turns green,
I see that the **ver** is on its way.
The sun beats down on the summer fields,
For the **aestas** has come with a sunny day.

<u>Caelum Song</u> [Audio File 26(C)/56(E)]

Luna moon and **stella** star,
How I wonder what you are.
Up above in the **caelum** high,
Like a diamond in the sky.
When the nighttime turns to day,
Then the **sol** comes out to stay.

Activities

1. Color each picture and add things to make it look like the right season. Think about the sky and the weather as you draw. Be ready to tell the Latin names for the things in your pictures!

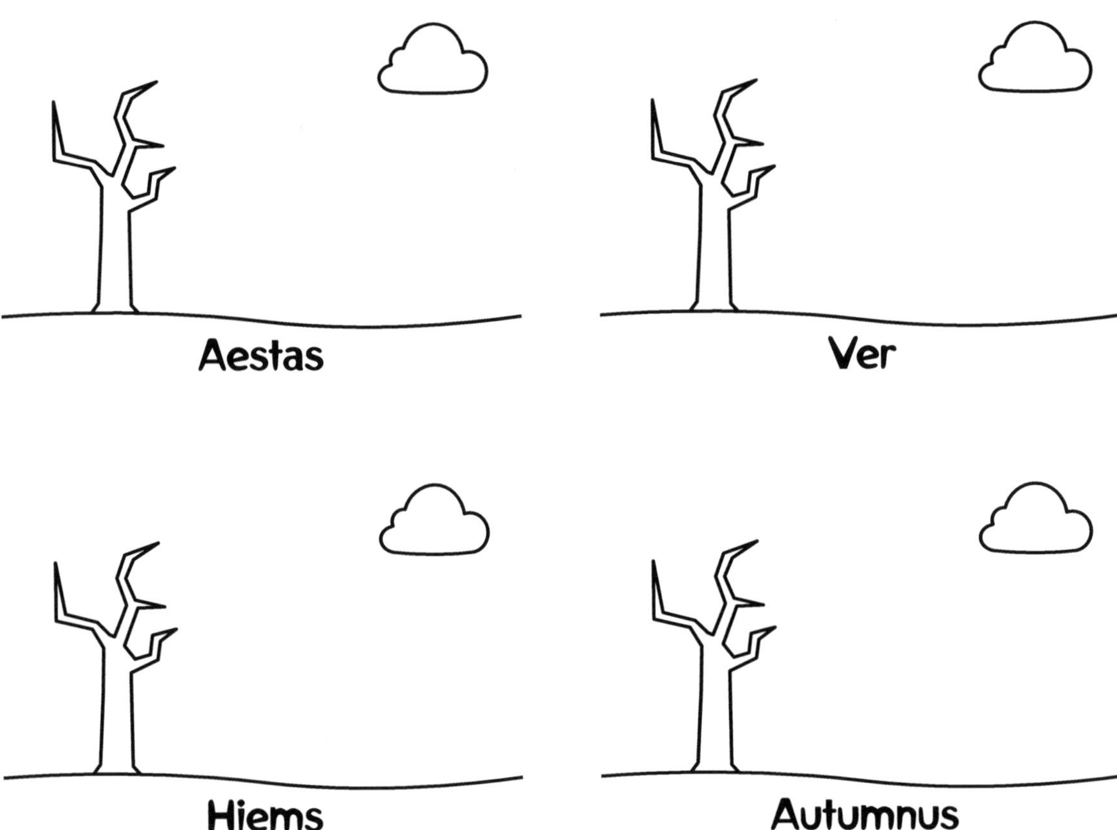

2. Draw a line from the pictures to the Latin words.

Chapter Story

<u>Joseph's Dream</u>

Once there was a **puer** named Joseph, and he lived with his eleven **fraters**. They were jealous of Joseph because he had a coat with all the colors of the **arcus**. They were mean to Joseph. One night, when everyone was in bed sleeping, Joseph had a strange dream. He dreamed that he was out in a field. It was **autumnus**, so he was harvesting wheat with his **fraters**. All of a sudden his bundle of wheat stood straight up, and his **fraters'** bundles of wheat all bowed down to his wheat! Then he had another dream. He dreamed that the **sol**, the **luna**, and eleven **stellas** all bowed down to him. When he told his dreams to his **fraters**, they were angry! "We will never bow to you like that!" they said. Even his **pater** agreed. But they were wrong.

One day, Joseph's **fraters** were so angry with him that they sold him as a slave. The slave traders took him very far away, to Egypt. Joseph was very sad and his life was very hard for a long time. Whenever he looked up in the night **caelum** and saw the **stellas** and **luna**, he remembered his dream. But he worked faithfully in the hot **sol** and **ventus**, or in the **imber**, and a few years later, Pharaoh made Joseph a very important ruler in Egypt. He was in charge of almost everything and he lived in the palace. He helped the people store up **cibus** before a famine.

One **ver** day, he saw his **fraters** coming to get **cibus**! They bowed down to him, just like the **sol**, **luna**, and **stellas** had done in Joseph's dream. Joseph forgave them for being so unkind to him. He gave them the **cibus** they needed. Soon after that, his whole family came to live with him in Egypt. They were very happy to be together again!

–*Adapted from Genesis 37 & 42*

Chapter 28

Water Words

Words to Learn

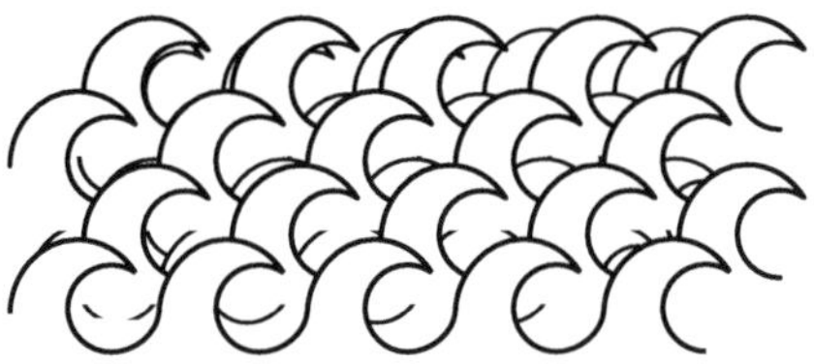

1. **mare** sea
2. **unda** wave
3. **lacus** lake
4. **flumen** river
5. **navis** ship/boat

Chapter Song

Row Your Navis [Audio File 27(C)/57(E)]

Navis, navis – boat,
Mare, mare – sea.
Ride the **unda**, ride the wave,
Happy as can be.

Lacus, lacus – lake,
Flumen – river, stream.
Row your **navis**, row your boat,
Life is but a dream.

Chapter Lesson

Did you notice that all of your new words this week are related to water? If you like boats and playing in water, you will have a lot of fun with these words! Have you ever been in a **navis**? Have you ever gone tubing on a **flumen** or fishing on a **lacus**?

Famous Latin Saying

If you live in America, do you know what country your ancestors lived in before they came to the United States? Can you tell what English word comes from **pluribus** (from Chapter 26's phrase)? The word "plural," which means many or more than one. If you add an "s" to most nouns you make it plural (like "state" and "states"). Though there are many waves, there is just one…**mare**.

Grow Your English

A navy is a part of the military that mainly operates on the water. The United States Navy has many, many ships! What Latin word do you think navy came from?

Practice Your Latin

1. Practice writing your new words by tracing the dots.

Mare Unda Lacus

Flumen Navis

2. Turn to page 131 and follow the directions to make a **navis**. Be sure to sail it when you sing the song!

3. Using the pictures below, follow the instructions to draw the correct Latin words.

a. Draw a **piscis** in the **unda**.

b. Draw a bridge over the **flumen**.

c. Draw a **navis** on the **lacus**.

4. Circle the word that fits best.

a. The Nile _________ is in Egypt.

lacus **flumen** **navis**

b. A _________ knocked me over when I went to the ocean.

navis **unda** **flumen**

c. I sailed around Africa in my _________.

lacus **mare** **navis**

d. Seahorses live in the _________.

flumen **mare** **lacus**

e. The lake house is beside the _________.

lacus **unda** **navis**

Show What You Know

Match the Latin word to the English word.

1. **navis**	wave
2. **lacus**	ship/boat
3. **mare**	river
4. **unda**	lake
5. **flumen**	sea

Review:

Match the Latin word to the English word.

1. **cano**	shepherd
2. **laudo**	lamb
3. **agnus**	I praise
4. **pastor**	I sing

Chapter 29

Gardening

Words to Learn

1. **flos** flower
2. **herba** plant
3. **hortus** garden
4. **folium** leaf
5. **humus** ground/dirt

Chapter Song

<u>Hortus Song</u> [Audio File 28(C)/58(E)]

Grab your shovel,
Put your gloves on,
It's time to plant our summer **hortus**.
Here's a **herba**, plant,
With a **folium**, a leaf,
Let's plant it in our summer **hortus**.

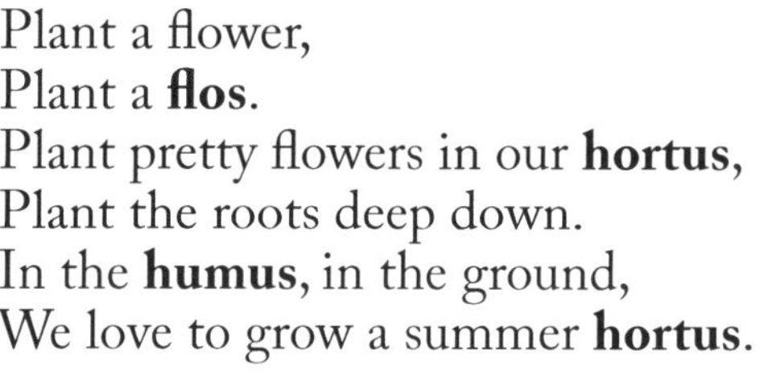

Plant a flower,
Plant a **flos**.
Plant pretty flowers in our **hortus**,
Plant the roots deep down.
In the **humus**, in the ground,
We love to grow a summer **hortus**.

Chapter Lesson

Have you ever helped to plant a garden? Even if you have not, you have seen many things growing. It is amazing to see how a tiny seed can grow into a plant or a big tree, and even produce food for us to eat. Next time you go outside, notice all the things that are growing, and call as many as you can by their Latin names.

<u>Famous Latin Saying</u>

When you make a mistake, you can simply say, "Sorry, **mea culpa**!" **Mea culpa** means "my fault." If you accidently poured **aqua** on your **feles**, you should say "**Mea culpa**!" to your cat.

Practice Your Latin

1. Practice writing your new words by tracing the dots.

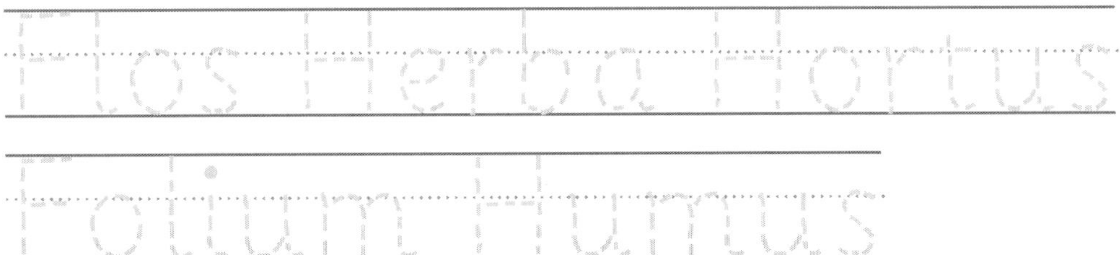

2. Draw your garden and connect the vocabulary words to the things in your garden.

flos **herba** **hortus** **folium** **humus**

3. Circle the word that fits best.

a. Till the _________ before you plant a garden!

folium	**humus**	**herba**

b. Pick a _________ for your mother.

humus	**herba**	**flos**

c. The _________ on the tree changes colors in the fall.

folium	**hortus**	**arbor**

d. We grow a lot of vegetables in our _________.

folium	**hortus**	**herba**

e. I pick tomatoes off of the tomato _________.

humus	**folium**	**herba**

Show What You Know

Circle the correct English definition of these Latin words.

1. **hortus**	garden	plant	flower
2. **herba**	leaf	flower	plant
3. **humus**	flower	garden	ground/dirt
4. **flos**	plant	flower	leaf
5. **folium**	leaf	ground/dirt	plant

Review

Circle the correct English definition of these Latin words.

1. **lacus**	summer	river	lake
2. **navis**	river	ship/boat	winter
3. **hiems**	winter	lake	spring
4. **aestas**	fall	winter	summer

Chapter 30 Playing Outdoors

Words to Learn

1. **mons** mountain
2. **arbor** tree
3. **saxum** rock
4. **collis** hill
5. **silva** forest

Chapter Song

Hiking Song [Audio File 29(C)/59(E)]

Climb the mountain, climb the mountain,
Mountain – **mons**! Mountain – **mons**!
Throw a **saxum**, throw a **saxum**,
Saxum – rock! **Saxum** – rock!

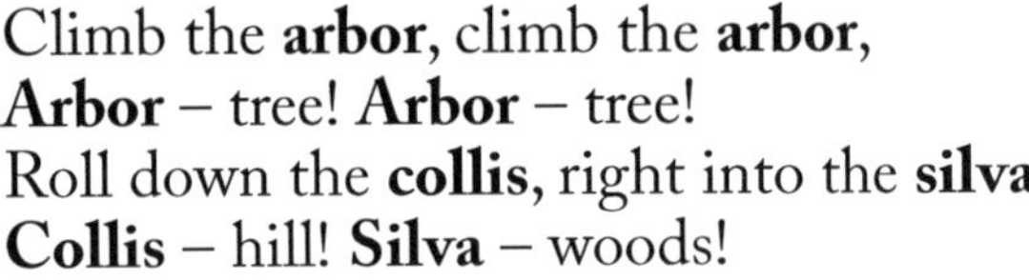

Climb the **arbor**, climb the **arbor**,
Arbor – tree! **Arbor** – tree!
Roll down the **collis**, right into the **silva**,
Collis – hill! **Silva** – woods!

Chapter Lesson

You have five outdoor words to learn this week. Think about and practice these words whenever you go outside! You probably at least see an **arbor** every day. You probably see a **saxum**, too. If you throw a **saxum**, make sure nothing is in the way! All of the words in this chapter are nouns. Do you remember how you find nouns that are in the first declension? (They end with an *a*.) Can you tell which of your new words is a first declension noun?

Famous Latin Saying

If you have ever spent a long time on a boat, it usually feels good when you finally arrive to shore and can put your feet on **terra firma**—"solid ground." People often use the phrase **terra firma** to say that something is strong and solid, even when they don't really mean the ground. For example, somone might say, "I did not understand my math homework until my sister explained it to me. Now I feel that I am on **terra firma**." From **firma** we get our word "firm."

Practice Your Latin

1. Practice writing your new words by tracing the dots.

Mons Arbor Saxum

Collis Silva

2. Label your pictures with the Latin words.

a. Draw a **saxum** on a **collis**.

b. Draw an **arbor** on a **mons**.

c. Draw a **silva**.

3. Look at the pictures and fill in the correct Latin word to complete the sentences, choosing from the words in the box.

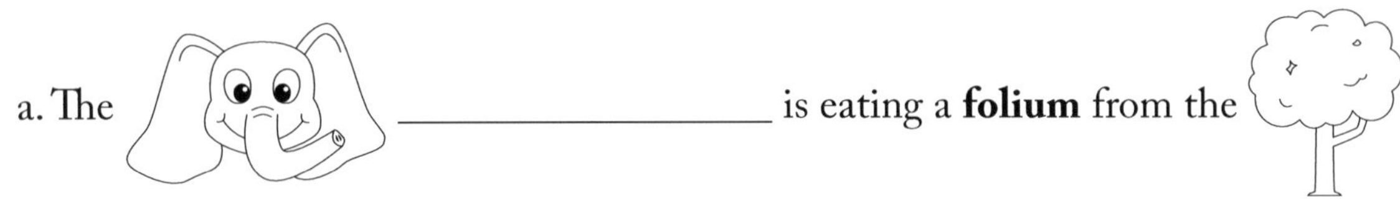

a. The ____________________ is eating a **folium** from the

____________________.

b. The bear is hiding in the ____________________.

c. The **vir** is climbing the big ____________________.

d. The **puer** found a new ____________________ on the road to add to his collection.

e. The children are sledding down the ____________________ in the snow.

saxum	**collis**	**elephantus**	**mons**	**silva**	**arbor**

Show What You Know

Match the Latin words to the English words.

1. **saxum** tree

2. **arbor** hill

3. **mons** rock

4. **collis** forest

5. **silva** mountain

Review

Match the Latin words to the English words.

1. **manus** body

2. **corpus** eye

3. **auris** hand

4. **os** ear

5. **oculus** mouth

Chapter 31

Review

Chapter 28 Words

1. mare ______________________
2. unda ______________________
3. lacus ______________________
4. flumen ______________________
5. navis ______________________

Chapter 29 Words

1. flos ______________________
2. herba ______________________
3. hortus ______________________
4. folium ______________________
5. humus ______________________

Chapter 30 Words

1. mons ______________________
2. arbor ______________________
3. saxum ______________________
4. collis ______________________
5. silva ______________________

Master Your Songs

Row Your Navis [Audio File 27(C)/57(E)]

Navis, navis – boat,
Mare, mare – sea.
Ride the **unda**, ride the wave,
Happy as can be.

Lacus, lacus – lake,
Flumen – river, stream.
Row your **navis**, row your boat,
Life is but a dream.

Hortus Song [Audio File 28(C)/58(E)]

Grab your shovel,
Put your gloves on,
It's time to plant our summer **hortus**.
Here's an **herba**, plant,
With a **folium**, a leaf,
Let's plant it in our summer **hortus**.

Plant a flower,
Plant a **flos**.
Plant pretty flowers in our **hortus**,
Plant the roots deep down.
In the **humus**, in the ground,
We love to grow a summer **hortus**.

Hiking Song [Audio File 29(C)/59(E)]

Climb the mountain, climb the mountain,
Mountain – **mons**! Mountain – **mons**!
Throw a **saxum**, throw a **saxum**,
Saxum - rock! **Saxum** – rock!

Climb the arbor, Climb the arbor,
Arbor – tree! **Arbor** – tree!
Roll down the **collis**, right into the **silva**,
Collis - hill! **Silva** – woods!

__Sailing Song__ [Audio File 30(C)/60(E)]
Here is another song you can listen to to help you remember the water words.

As I sailed out on the wide open **mare,**
I sailed on the **mare** as free as could be.
I spied a huge **unda** about to wash o'er me,
An **unda** of **aqua** out on the wide sea.

I cast off my **navis** to fish in the **flumen,**
Fish in the **flumen** one warm summer night.
The river, it took me right out to the **lacus,**
And there on the **lacus** I got my first bite.

Activities

1. Label all the key items in this scene.

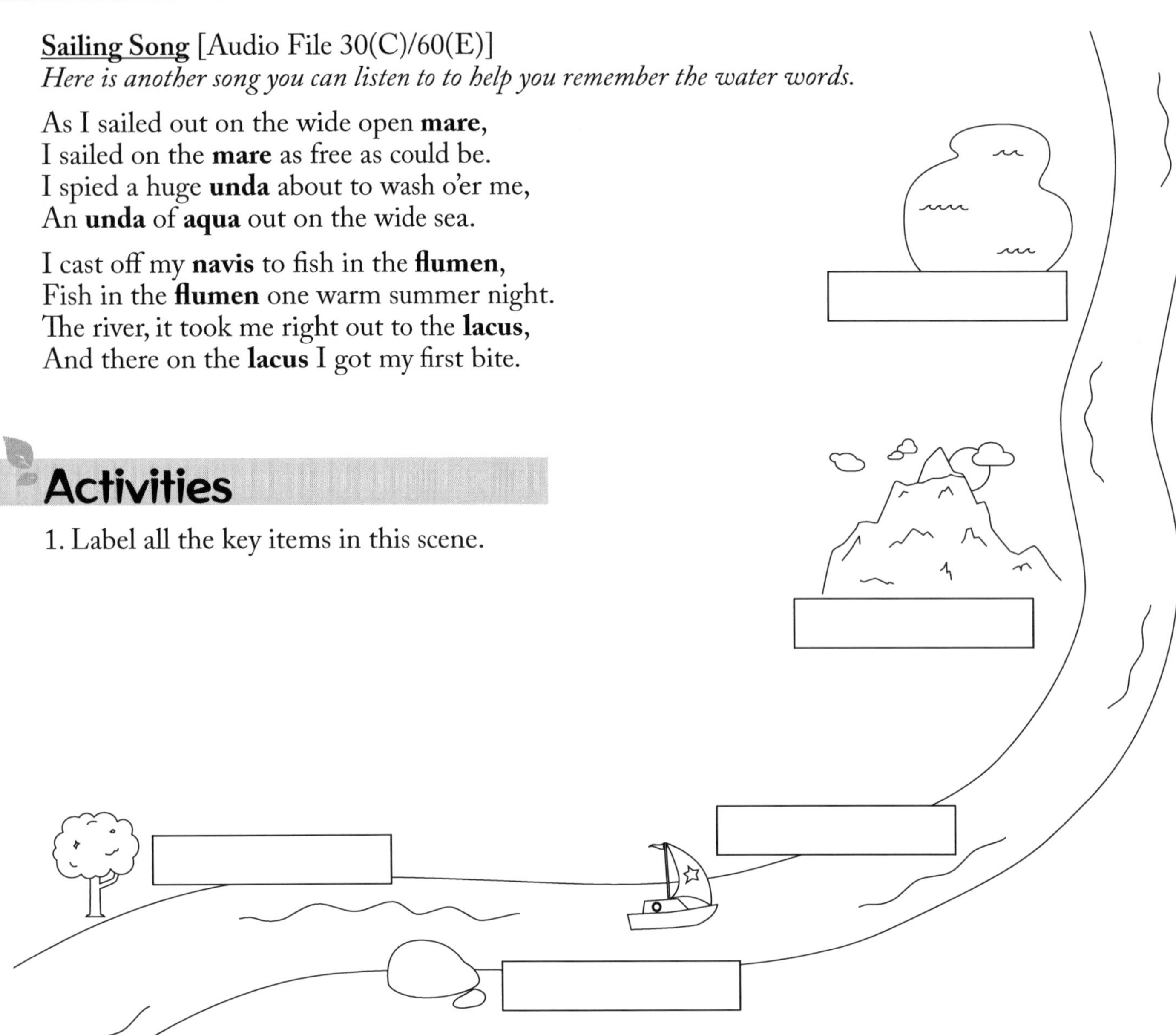

2. Look at the pictures and fill in the correct Latin word to complete the sentences, choosing from the words in the box.

Flos
Flumen
Herba
Lacus
Saxum
Arbor
Hortus
Mons
Piscis

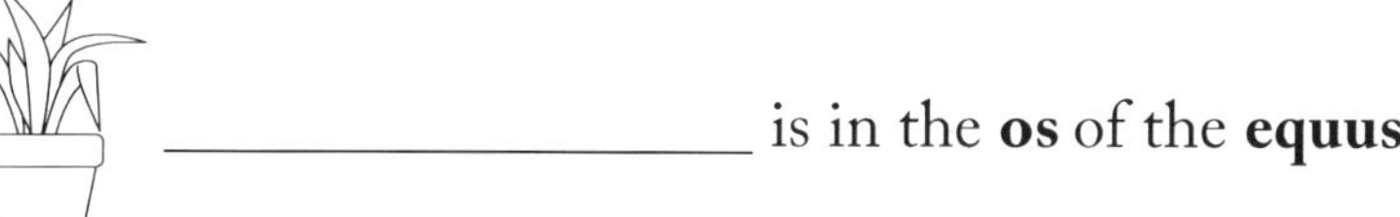

a. The ____________________ is in the **os** of the **equus**.

b. The **avis** is in the ____________________.

c. The **feles** is looking at the ____________________.

d. The **puella** is sitting on the ____________________.

e. There is a ____________________ in the girl's hair.

f. The **canis** is swimming in the ____________________.

g. The **femina** is working in the ____________________.

h. You can see a ____________________ behind the **hortus**.

i. There is a ____________________ floating in the little ____________________.

3. What do you think you would see if you took a hike in the **silva**? Draw a picture with three things that you can name in Latin.

4. Draw a line from each item to the place where you would see normally see it—water or dry ground.

Appendix A

Chapter-by-Chapter Glossary

Chapter 1: Greeting Words

1. **salve**	hello
2. **vale**	good-bye
3. **discipuli**	students
4. **magister/magistra**	teacher

Chapter 2: Making Friends

1. **Quid est tuum praenomen?**
   What is your name?
2. **Meum praenomen est…**
   My name is...

Chapter 3: How Are You?

1. **Quid agis?**	How are you?
2. **sum**	I am
3. **bene**	well/fine
4. **optime**	great
5. **pessime**	terrible

Chapter 5: Family Members

1. **pater**	father
2. **mater**	mother
3. **soror**	sister
4. **frater**	brother

Chapter 6: People

1. **puella**	girl
2. **puer**	boy
3. **vir**	man
4. **femina**	woman

Chapter 7: Classroom Items

1. **mensa**	table
2. **sella**	chair
3. **stylus**	pencil
4. **liber**	book

Chapter 8: Household Items

1. **casa**	house
2. **porta**	door
3. **murus**	wall
4. **fenestra**	window

Chapter 10: Classroom Commands

1. **sede**	sit
sedete	sit (more than 1 person)
2. **surge**	rise/stand up
surgite	rise/stand up (more than 1 person)
3. **scribe**	write
scribite	write (more than 1 person)
4. **repete**	repeat
repetite	repeat (more than 1 person)

Chapter 11: More Classroom Commands

1. **audi**	listen
audite	listen (more than 1 person)
2. **tace**	be quiet
tacete	be quiet (more than 1 person)
3. **aperi librum**	open the book
aperite libros	open the books (more than 1 person)
4. **attole manum**	raise your hand
attolite manus	raise your hands (more than 1 person)

Be sure to test your skills in the End-of-Year Crossword on page 133!

Chapter 12: Manners

1. **amabo te**	please
2. **tibi gratias ago**	thank you
3. **ignosce mihi**	excuse me

Chapter 14: Pets

1. **canis**	dog
2. **feles**	cat
3. **equus**	horse
4. **piscis**	fish

Chapter 15: Animals

1. **leo**	lion
2. **avis**	bird
3. **ursa**	bear
4. **elephantus**	elephant

Chapter 16: Christmas Words

1. **angelus**	angel
2. **pastor**	shepherd
3. **agnus**	lamb
4. **stella**	star
5. **infans**	baby

Chapter 17: More Christmas Words

1. **cano**	I sing
2. **laudo**	I praise
3. **do**	I give
4. **donum**	gift

Chapter 19: The Body

1. **manus**	hand
2. **pes**	foot
3. **caput**	head
4. **corpus**	body

Chapter 20: The Face

1. **auris**	ear
2. **nares**	nose
3. **oculus**	eye
4. **os**	mouth

Chapter 21: Food Words

1. **cibus**	food
2. **aqua**	water
3. **cena**	dinner
4. **edo**	I eat
5. **bibo**	I drink

Chapter 22: More Food Words

1. **panis**	bread
2. **fructus**	fruit
3. **lac**	milk
4. **crustulum**	cookie
5. **pullus**	chicken

Chapter 24: Weather

1. **nix**	snow
2. **imber**	rain
3. **ventus**	wind
4. **nimbus**	cloud
5. **arcus**	rainbow

Chapter 25: The Seasons

1. **hiems** winter
2. **ver** spring
3. **autumnus** fall
4. **aestas** summer

Chapter 26: The Sky

1. **caelum** sky
2. **luna** moon
3. **stella** star
4. **sol** sun

Chapter 28: Water Words

1. **mare** sea
2. **unda** wave
3. **lacus** lake
4. **flumen** river
5. **navis** ship/boat

Chapter 29: Gardening

1. **flos** flower
2. **herba** plant
3. **hortus** garden
4. **folium** leaf
5. **humus** ground/dirt

Chapter 30: Playing Outdoors

1. **mons** mountain
2. **arbor** tree
3. **saxum** rock
4. **collis** hill
5. **silva** forest

Appendix B

Alphabetical Glossary

aestas . . . . summer
agnus . . . . lamb
amabo te. . . . . please
angelus. . . . . angel
aperi librum . . . . open the book
aperite libros . . . . open the books
(more than 1 person)
aqua . . . . water
arbor. . . . . tree
arcus. . . . . rainbow
attole manum. . . . . raise your hand
attolite manus . . . . raise your hands
(more than 1 person)
audi . . . . listen
audite. . . . . listen
(more than 1 person)
auris . . . . ear
autumnus. . . . . fall
avis. . . . . bird
bene . . . . well/fine
bibo . . . . I drink
caelum . . . . sky
canis. . . . . dog
cano . . . . I sing
caput . . . . head
casa. . . . . house
cena . . . . dinner
cibus. . . . . food
collis. . . . . hill
corpus . . . . body
crustulum. . . . . cookie
discipuli . . . . students
do . . . . I give
donum . . . . gift
edo . . . . I eat
elephantus . . . . elephant
equus . . . . horse
feles . . . . cat
femina . . . . woman
fenestra . . . . window
flos . . . . flower
flumen . . . . river
folium . . . . leaf
frater . . . . brother
fructus . . . . fruit
herba . . . . plant
hiems . . . . winter
hortus. . . . . garden
humus . . . . ground/dirt
ignosce mihi. . . . . excuse me
imber . . . . rain
infans . . . . baby
iratus . . . . angry
lac. . . . . milk
lacus . . . . lake
laudo . . . . I praise
leo. . . . . lion
liber . . . . book
luna . . . . moon
magister/magistra . . . . . . teacher
manus. . . . . hand
mare . . . . sea
mater . . . . mother
mensa. . . . . table
Meum praenomen est… . My name is...

mons . . . . mountain
murus . . . . wall
nares . . . . nose
navis . . . . ship/boat
nimbus . . . . cloud
nix . . . . snow
oculus . . . . eye
optime . . . . great
os . . . . mouth
panis . . . . bread
pastor . . . . shepherd
pater . . . . father
pes . . . . foot
pessime . . . . terrible
piscis . . . . fish
porta . . . . door
puella . . . . girl
puer . . . . boy
pullus . . . . chicken
Quid agis? . . . . How are you?
Quid est tuum praenomen? . . . . What is your name?
repete . . . . repeat
repetite . . . . repeat (more than 1 person)
salve . . . . hello
saxum . . . . rock
scribe . . . . write
scribite . . . . write (more than 1 person)
sede . . . . sit
sedete . . . . sit (more than 1 person)
sella . . . . chair
silva . . . . forest
sol . . . . sun
soror . . . . sister
stella . . . . star
stylus . . . . pencil
sum . . . . I am
surge . . . . rise/stand up
surgite . . . . rise/stand up (more than 1 person)
tace . . . . be quiet
tacete . . . . be quiet (more than 1 person)
tibi gratias ago . . . . thank you
unda . . . . wave
tristis . . . . sad
ursa . . . . bear
vale . . . . good-bye
ventus . . . . wind
ver . . . . spring
vir . . . . man

These cutouts accompany the exercise on page 19.

These cutouts accompany the exercise on page 22.

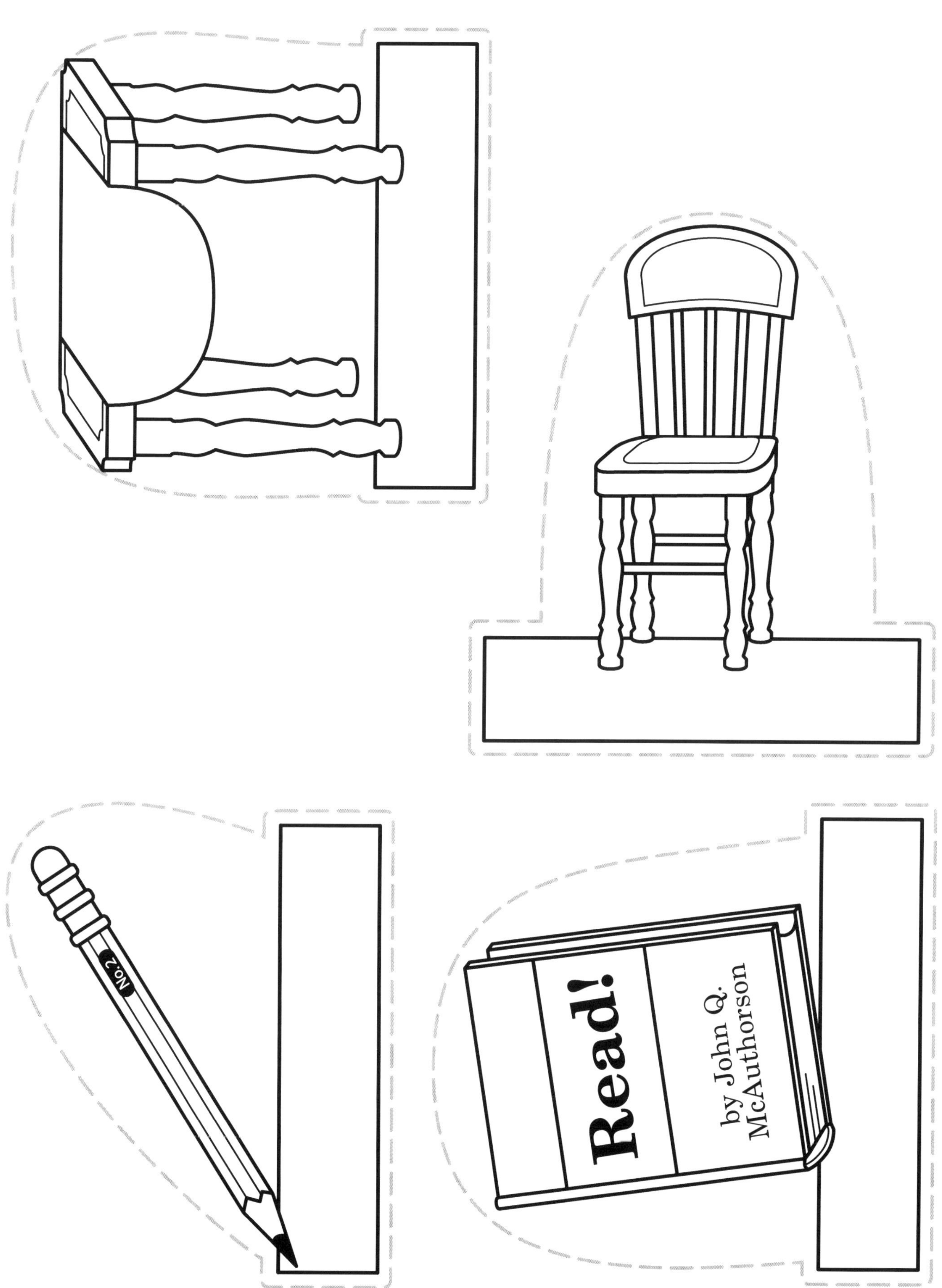

These cutouts accompany the exercise on page 78.

These cutouts accompany the exercise on page 87.

These cutouts accompany the exercise on page 92.

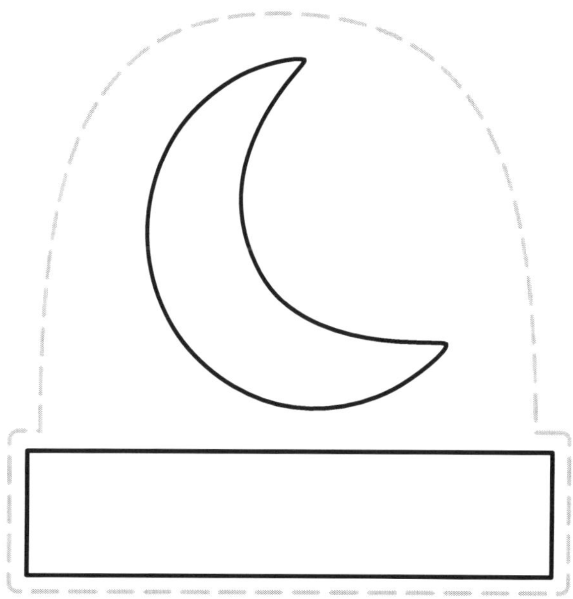

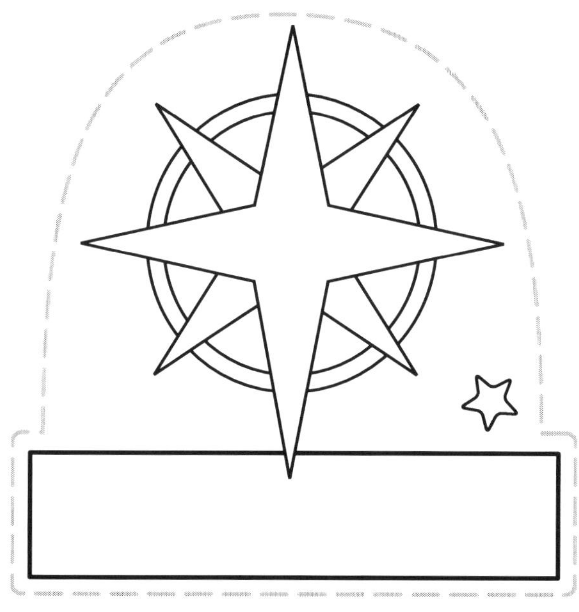

Day

Night

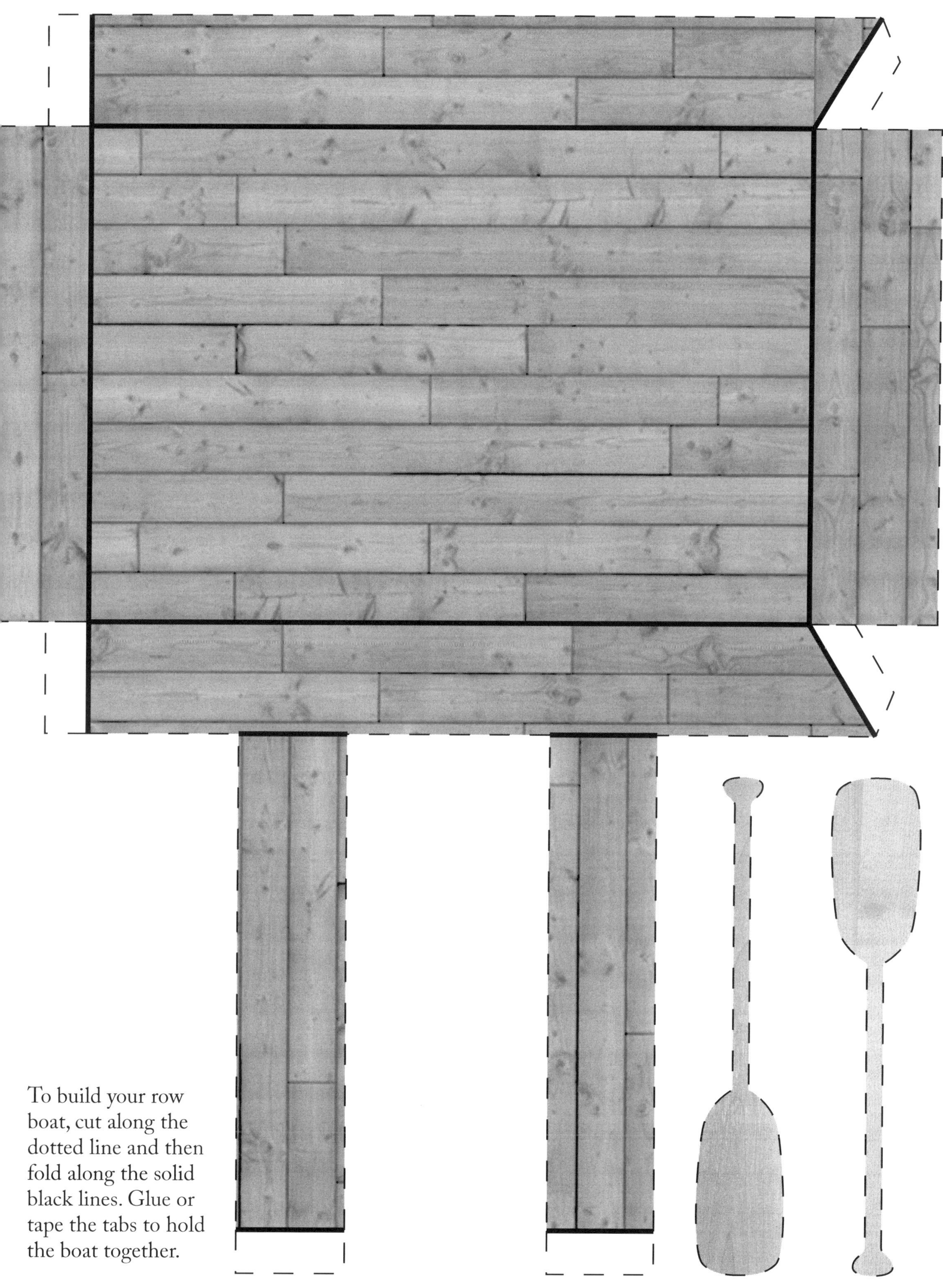

To build your row boat, cut along the dotted line and then fold along the solid black lines. Glue or tape the tabs to hold the boat together.

End-of-Year Crossword

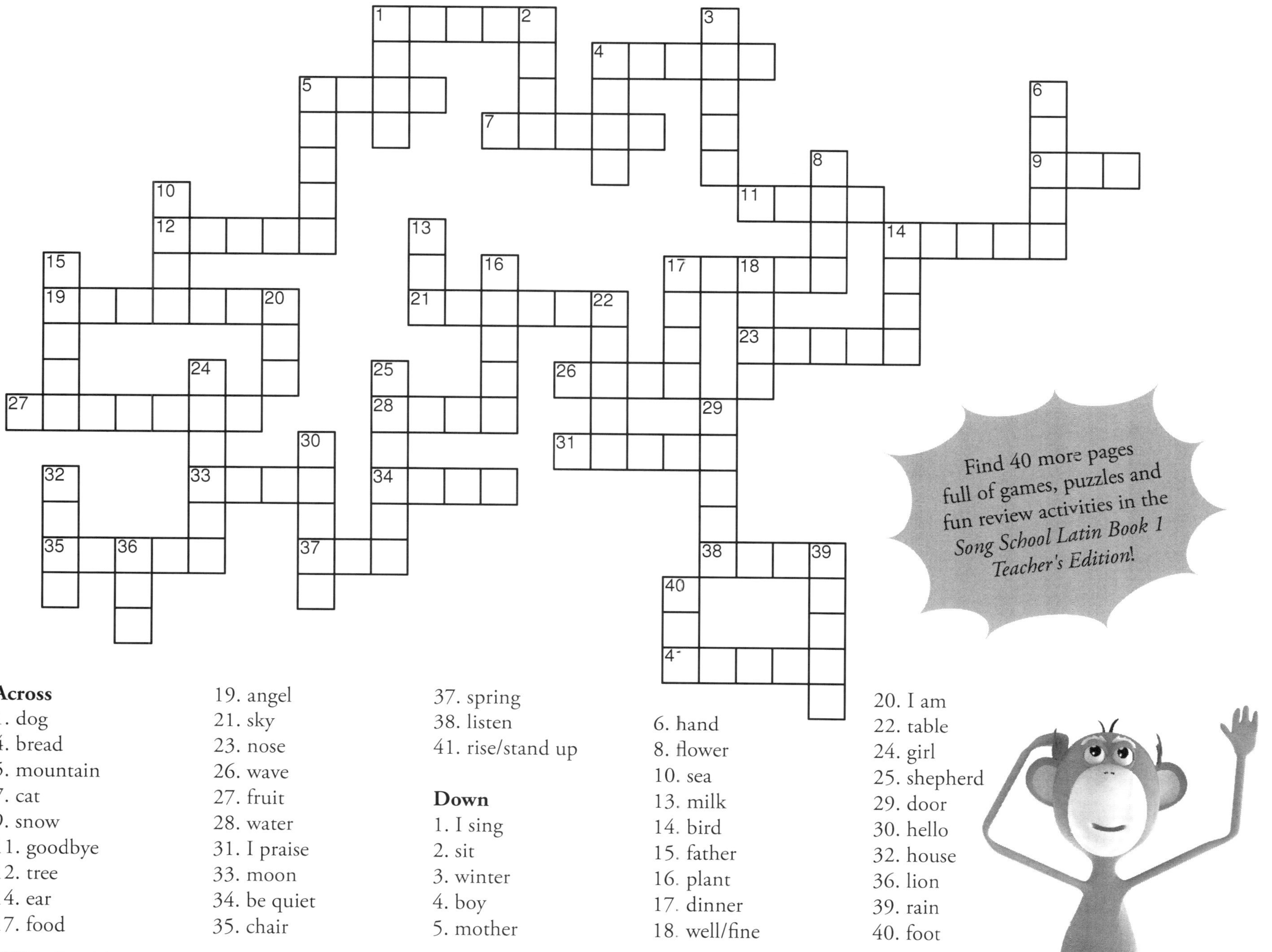

Across
1. dog
4. bread
5. mountain
7. cat
9. snow
11. goodbye
12. tree
14. ear
17. food
19. angel
21. sky
23. nose
26. wave
27. fruit
28. water
31. I praise
33. moon
34. be quiet
35. chair
37. spring
38. listen
41. rise/stand up

Down
1. I sing
2. sit
3. winter
4. boy
5. mother
6. hand
8. flower
10. sea
13. milk
14. bird
15. father
16. plant
17. dinner
18. well/fine
20. I am
22. table
24. girl
25. shepherd
29. door
30. hello
32. house
36. lion
39. rain
40. foot

Your Latin Journey

Lower Grammar

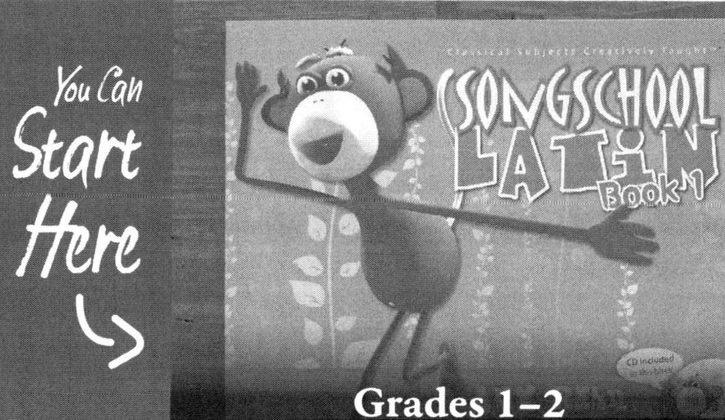

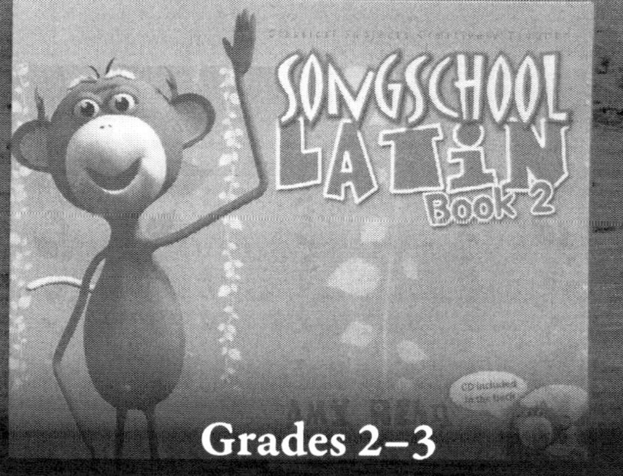

Upper Grammar

Middle & High School

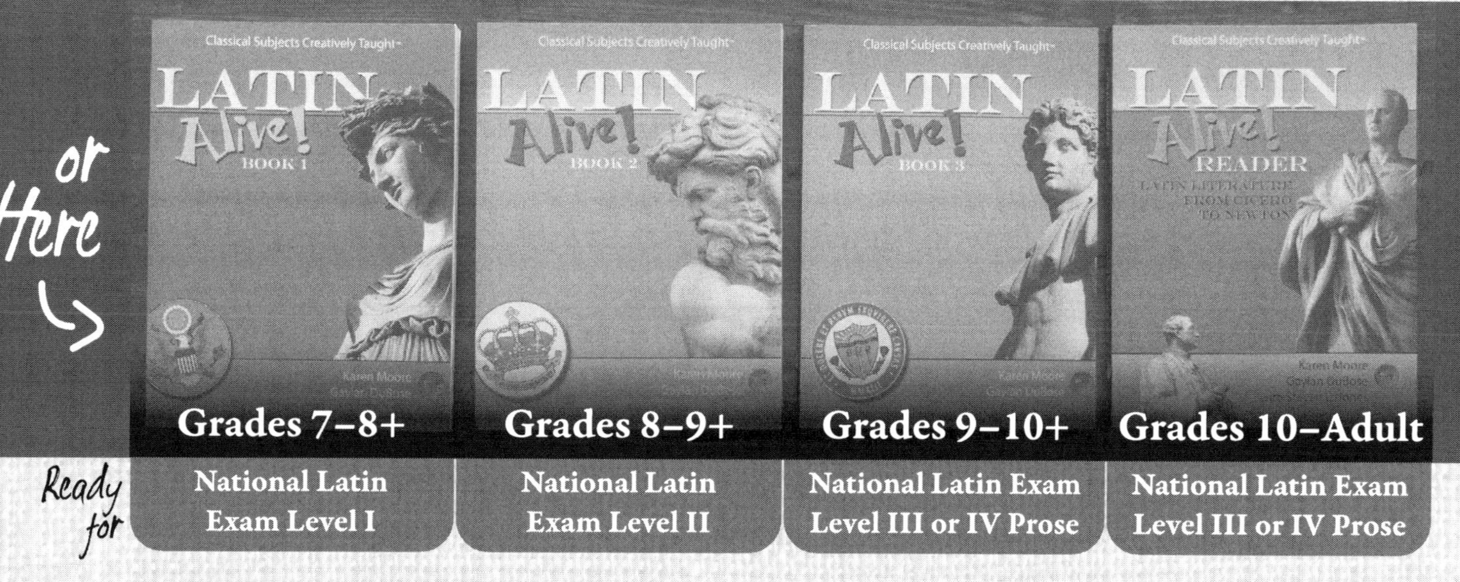